THE HISTORY OF SCOTLAND FOR CHILDREN

*

Judy Paterson

ILLUSTRATED BY
Sally J. Collins

GLOWWORM BOOKS LTD

THE HISTORY OF SCOTLAND FOR CHILDREN

Dedication

To Mike,

who made it possible

Acknowledgements and Author's Note

Political intrigue, national and international, the complexities of religious trends, social mores, wars,
assassinations as well as deeds of great bravery make up the warp on the loom of history. Threaded throughout are those
who make up the weft: kings and queens, servants and slaves, the rich and the poor, the brave and the imaginative. The pattern
which emerges is a portrait of a nation's people. My story of Scotland can only be a concise introduction
to the main events and some of the people in Scottish history.

To present such a rich and varied history in one volume suitable for children has been a challenge.
In researching and writing this book I have met with enthusiastic support, help, criticism, encouragement and advice.
To the late James Drummond, I owe special thanks. His invaluable advice and criticism shaped an
unweildy manuscript and his warm encouragement was much appreciated.

My thanks to Francis Jarvie for her editorial work and to Joyce Barnes, School Library Development Officer,
West Lothian, for helpful comment and advice. Thanks also to Sheila Maher of James Thin Booksellers, Edinburgh.
My gratitude is extended to the staff of Historic Scotland, the National Trust for Scotland and the Museum of Scotland. In
particular, I wish to thank David Hendrie, Historic Scotland Photographic Unit for the use of his photographs of the Bruce
Heart Casket and the Commemorative Plaque which we have used on the title page.

Thanks also to Phil Rogers of the Scottish Office Information Directorate, and to the Scottish Hydro-Electric PLC which
kindly supplied a difficult-to find photograph of Tom Johnston. Also thanks to Norma Rutherford for pictures of the return of
the Stone of Destiny at Coldstream, and to James G Henderson, MBE NUJ, of Golspie for material on the Clearances.
I have used many libraries in the course of preparation but would like to thank the staff at Inverkeithing Library, especially.

Thanks to friends and family for all they have done to help. To Alec Talbot of Adelaide, Australia, a headmaster who inspired
me as a teacher and then believed in me, thank you. To Frank Hepburn, a friend whose deep interest in literature and history is
always stimulating, I owe thanks for much, including the use of some rare books. Sally J. Collins has been more than an illus-
trator. She has inspired me, edited text and been a confidante. My thanks to all the children I have taught in the past, especially
those who asked "why" and "how". Finally, the realisation of this project is due to the unique support of my husband, Mike, to
whom I dedicate this book with love and thanks.

Text © Judy Paterson
Illustrations © Sally J. Collins

First published in 1999 by
Glowworm Books Ltd. Unit 7, Greendykes Industrial Estate,
Broxburn, West Lothian, EH52 6PG, Scotland

Reprinted 2000

Telephone: 01506-857570
Fax: 01506-858100
E-Mail: admin@glowwormbooks.co.uk
URL: http://www.glowwormbooks.co.uk

ISBN 1-871512-63-8 (paperback)
ISBN 1-871512-56-5 (hardback)

Printed and bound in Scotland

Page layout by Mark Blackadder

Reprint Code   10   9   8   7   6   5   4   3   2

THE
HISTORY OF
SCOTLAND
FOR CHILDREN

CONTENTS

SCOTTISH HISTORY TIMELINE

This shows the main events which made Scotland a nation. It highlights Scotland's fight to maintain its identity and freedom.

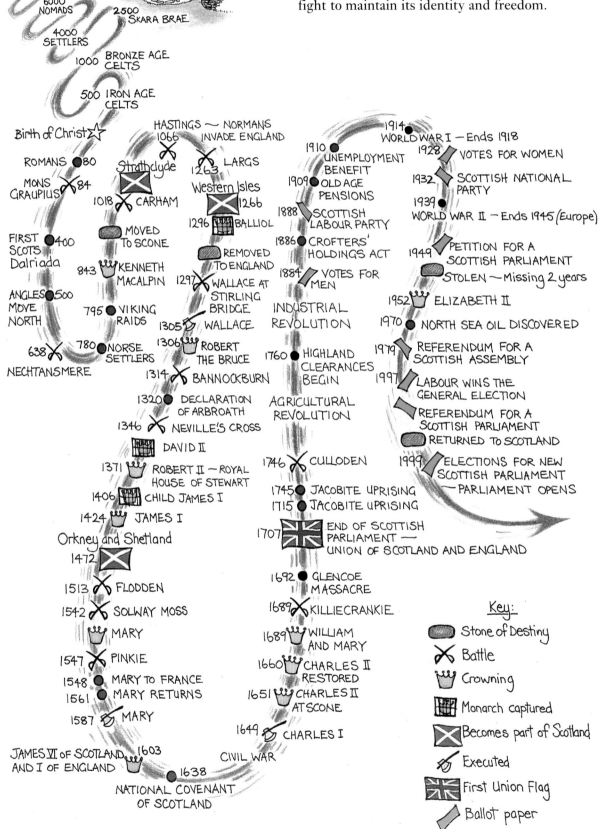

STONE AGE
6000 NOMADS
4000 SETTLERS
2500 SKARA BRAE
1000 BRONZE AGE CELTS
500 IRON AGE CELTS

Birth of Christ
ROMANS 80
MONS GRAUPIUS 84
Strathclyde
1018 CARHAM
HASTINGS ~ NORMANS INVADE ENGLAND 1066
1263 LARGS
Western Isles 1266
1296 BALLIOL
MOVED TO SCONE
FIRST SCOTS Dalriada 400
843 KENNETH MACALPIN
REMOVED TO ENGLAND
1297 WALLACE AT STIRLING BRIDGE
ANGLES MOVE NORTH 500
795 VIKING RAIDS
1305 WALLACE
638 NECHTANSMERE
780 NORSE SETTLERS
1306 ROBERT THE BRUCE
1314 BANNOCKBURN
1320 DECLARATION OF ARBROATH
1346 NEVILLE'S CROSS
DAVID II
1371 ROBERT II — ROYAL HOUSE OF STEWART
1406 CHILD JAMES I
1424 JAMES I
Orkney and Shetland 1472
1513 FLODDEN
1542 SOLWAY MOSS
MARY
1547 PINKIE
1548 MARY TO FRANCE
1561 MARY RETURNS
1587 MARY
JAMES VI OF SCOTLAND AND I OF ENGLAND 1603
1638 NATIONAL COVENANT OF SCOTLAND
CIVIL WAR
1649 CHARLES I
1651 CHARLES II AT SCONE
1660 CHARLES II RESTORED
1689 WILLIAM AND MARY
1689 KILLIECRANKIE
1692 GLENCOE MASSACRE
1707 END OF SCOTTISH PARLIAMENT — UNION OF SCOTLAND AND ENGLAND
1715 JACOBITE UPRISING
1745 JACOBITE UPRISING
1746 CULLODEN
AGRICULTURAL REVOLUTION
1760 HIGHLAND CLEARANCES BEGIN
INDUSTRIAL REVOLUTION
1884 VOTES FOR MEN
1886 CROFTERS' HOLDINGS ACT
1888 SCOTTISH LABOUR PARTY
1909 OLD AGE PENSIONS
1910 UNEMPLOYMENT BENEFIT
1914 WORLD WAR I — Ends 1918
1928 VOTES FOR WOMEN
1932 SCOTTISH NATIONAL PARTY
1939 WORLD WAR II — Ends 1945 (Europe)
1949 PETITION FOR A SCOTTISH PARLIAMENT
STOLEN ~ Missing 2 years
1952 ELIZABETH II
1970 NORTH SEA OIL DISCOVERED
1979 REFERENDUM FOR A SCOTTISH ASSEMBLY
1997 LABOUR WINS THE GENERAL ELECTION
REFERENDUM FOR A SCOTTISH PARLIAMENT
RETURNED TO SCOTLAND
1999 ELECTIONS FOR NEW SCOTTISH PARLIAMENT — PARLIAMENT OPENS

Key:
Stone of Destiny
Battle
Crowning
Monarch captured
Becomes part of Scotland
Executed
First Union Flag
Ballot paper

SETTLERS AND INVADERS

THE STONE AGE
Nomads

The ice age lasted a long time in Scotland. The first visitors were Stone Age nomads. They were people who moved from one place to another searching for food. Between the years 6000 BC and 4000 BC, nomads came in boats during the summer months to fish and to hunt. It must have been like going on a holiday for the Stone Age people. Archaeologists have found campsites at places such as Morton on Tentsmuir in Fife.

Settlers

Later on, two things happened. Scotland became warmer and Stone Age people learnt about farming – growing crops, wheat and barley, and raising cattle, sheep and pigs for food. From about 4000 BC the first settlers decided to make their homes in Scotland. They settled mostly along the coastline and on the islands.

KEY: ● Settlements
      Coastline & Rivers

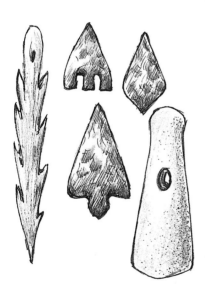

They left no written records. What we have learned about them comes from discovering artifacts. These are the tools they used. There are stone axe-heads, bone hooks for fishing and arrow-tips made from flint. Flint is a stone which can be chipped into sharp points. Archaeologists learn quite a bit from people's rubbish dumps too! They have also learned more about the way people lived from studying special sites such as Skara Brae and Jarlshof.

Skara Brae

Between 2500 BC and 2000 BC, settlers built a little village of ten houses at Skara Brae in Orkney. They built with stone because there were not many trees. Each one-roomed house had seats, beds and cupboards made of stone. They ate shellfish and seabirds and kept cattle and sheep. They made clothes from the hides of their animals. They made pots from clay, baked hard in peat fires. Many artifacts found here helped archaeologists and historians to learn about life in Skara Brae.

The village was buried in a sandstorm and it was only discovered after another great storm in 1866 AD. This means that Skara Brae is about 4,000 years old.

Jarlshof

On the southern point of Shetland stands another village dating back 4,000 years. Sir Walter Scott named it Jarlshof which was the name of the laird's house built there in the 17th Century. As with Skara Brae, severe storms in the 19th Century uncovered parts of earlier settlements.

At Jarlshof they built stone "wheelhouses" which were oval shaped and had roofs covered with turf. There was a main living-area with little rooms or alcoves all the way round. Some might have been storerooms while others might have been sleeping-quarters.

Later on, maybe for extra protection, some wheelhouses were built inside a round stone tower called a broch.

Jarlshof

Burial Sites, Standing Stones and the Beaker People

Stone Age people built cairns, mounds of stone, to make tombs for their dead relatives. The most important of these burial chambers is at Maes Howe in Orkney. Later settlers came to Scotland from the coast of Europe and buried their dead with a beaker, a pottery drinking vessel, which is why they were named Beaker people.

They are probably the people who built the Stone Circles. It is difficult to imagine how they were built and no-one really knows what they were for. They may have been religious meeting-places. In some circles the stones are placed to mark the moon's position in the sky at certain times of the year. There are 30 sites in Scotland. The most famous are the Stones

of Stenness and the Ring of Brogar in Orkney, and the Standing Stones at Callanish on Lewis.

Beaker people brought copper with them. They made the first metal weapons, daggers and axe-heads as well as tools and jewellery.

THE CELTS
Bronze Age Celts
Metal swords and shields of bronze were first made about 1000 BC in Europe. Bronze Age Celtic people migrated across Europe in search of land. People in Scotland traded their animal hides in Europe and brought back some of these new metal weapons. The Bronze Age Celts began to arrive in Scotland where they could take up farming.

Albion – The Scotland of about 700 BC
Good farming land was scarce and mostly found around the coastland. Family groups settled together so they could help and protect each other. Scotland as we know it was the northern part of a land known as Albion. People travelled by sea. It was easier than crossing the high mountains and boggy marshes which kept the northern part of Albion apart from the south. They traded with Ireland and with the countries on the east coast of Europe – Norway, Denmark, Germany, the Low Countries and France.

Albion's trading partners

Iron Age Celts
Sometime around 500 BC a new wave of Celts arrived in northern Albion. They wanted land for farming. Since most places were already settled, the only way they were going to get land was to take it. Because these Celts were great warriors, they usually got what they wanted.

When the Celts went into battle they used chariots pulled by fast ponies. They carried long spears and great leather shields and wore brightly coloured cloaks. Large war horns called carnyx, with dragon-like heads, were blown to frighten the enemy.

3

They had one great advantage over the Bronze Age people – iron. Their swords and spears were much stronger than weapons made of bronze. With these Celts came the Iron Age. Before long, the Celtic tribes, or family groups, settled in different parts of Albion, often fighting each other for land and cattle. They formed the early roots of the clan system. In the north of Albion one of these tribes was known as the Caledonians. The name, Caledonia, is still sometimes used for Scotland.

Protecting Homes and Land

Broch

A new way of living developed. The warrior Celts were also farmers and they built their small round houses inside a fortress so they could protect themselves against their enemies. Some fortresses were simply deep ditches with high wooden walls while others had stone walls and were called duns. They were mostly built on hill tops which made it easy to keep a look out over the countryside.

Dun

Some tribes living in the marshy lowlands defended themselves by building houses, called crannogs, which stood in the middle of lochs. In the far north where there are few trees, they built tall towers called brochs. Some historians think that brochs were built to protect people from the Romans who came to capture slaves.

On the land outside the fortress, the Celts cleared the forests and dug the ground with hoes. They grew small crops of corn and barley. They raised cattle, sheep, goats and pigs. They hunted deer and wild boar.

Celtic Crafts

Craftsmen had their workshops inside the fortress. The Celts loved beautiful things and they knew how to make fine gold jewellery, bracelets, brooches and torcs. They made mirrors from beaten bronze and hair combs from horn. Today many traditional Celtic designs are used in modern jewellery.

Crannog

The Blacksmith

The most important craftsman was the blacksmith. His workshop was a forge where he made iron, the strong metal that made swords and knives, wheel rims, blades for hoes, heads for hammers and axes. With the coming of iron the farmer's life was made easier.

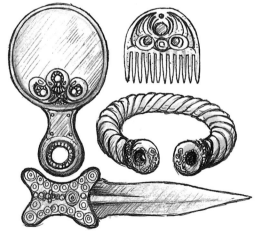

Celtic Crafts

Daily Life

The women ground corn in a small stone quern to make flour for baking bread and they brewed ale to drink. They cooked meat in a great bronze pot which hung from a chain over the fire which was in the middle of the house. Sometimes meat was roasted on a spit.

Most of what they wanted they made for themselves. They dyed wool with bright colours from lichen, roots and berries. The cloth they wove had designs of checks and stripes, the early forms of tartan. Women wore long tunics and cloaks while the men wore trousers, short tunics and "tartan" cloaks. Shoes, as well as warm clothes, were made from leather. The men used leather to make harnesses for their horses. The women also produced their own "make-up" from herbs and berries and they even made nail polish.

The Celts enjoyed feasts with music and storytelling. They had many gods and goddesses who, they believed, lived in lonely places in forests and beside streams and wells. The Celts believed their gods looked after their crops and their cattle, as well as bringing them victory in battle.

The First Highlanders

For hundreds of years the Celtic tribes lived in the glens and mountains of Northern Albion. The land had no king and the tribes were loyal only to their family and their chief. They traded in the south of Albion and with countries across the sea but, because they lived in a harsh land they were not rich. They were cut off from the rest of the country by mountains, rivers and marshes which made travel difficult. The land and the rugged coastline also kept enemies at bay.

KEY: Rivers, Lochs & Coastline
MMM Mountain Ranges

THE ROMANS

The Celtic tribes may have fought between themselves but when the Romans arrived they all faced a feared enemy. The Romans took over the south of Albion with a force of about 50,000 soldiers in the year 43 AD. They built roads and forts and captured slaves. Romans ruled the south which they called Britannia. Next they planned to conquer the north.

The Romans March North

In 80 AD the Romans reached the marshy Forth and Clyde valleys. The Romans built roads and forts to control the people who lived in the area.

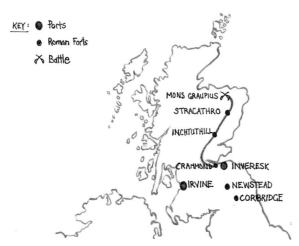

KEY: ● Ports
● Roman Forts
⚔ Battle

MONS GRAUPIUS ⚔
STRACATHRO ●
INCHTUTHILL ●
CRAMMOND ● ● INVERESK
● IRVINE ● NEWSTEAD
● CORBRIDGE

They built harbours at Inveresk on the Forth and Irvine on the west coast so that supplies from the south could reach the troops.

In 83 AD the Romans, led by Agricola, marched to conquer the far north. Although many different tribes lived here, the Romans called it the land of the Caledonians. Because of the rugged coastline on the west, the Romans had to march north on the eastern coast. They built forts, or "marching camps", along the way to try and stop the Caledonians attacking from the mountains. The Caledonians did attack. They came in small raiding parties and then quickly disappeared into the misty mountains. The Romans wanted to win an open battle. They wanted to conquer the Caledonians.

The Celts Fight Back

Finally, in 84 AD there was a battle. At Mons Graupius, somewhere near Elgin in Aberdeenshire, the Celtic tribes gathered. For the first time, the tribes forgot their differences

Mons Graupius

and joined forces to protect their homeland from the invaders. Their leader was named Calgacus. At the end of the battle the Romans wrote that they had lost about 300 men but they had killed about 10,000 Caledonians. Even so, they still did not gain control over the north.

The Celtic tribes returned to their glens and mountains and the Romans could not follow. They knew it was too difficult to control the tribes who lived in such a wild land. Though the Romans had conquered many parts of the world and the south of Albion, the north remained free.

The Roman Walls

Soon the Romans had to leave the Highlands because their soldiers were needed to fight in other parts of Europe. To protect the south, Britannia, from the raiding parties of the Caledonians, they decided to cut Britannia off from the north by building a great wall. They named it after Hadrian, the Emperor of Rome.

Hadrian's Wall of stone was begun in 120 AD. It stretched across the country from the Solway Firth to Wallsend on the River Tyne. It was really a raised roadway with fortresses where the Romans could keep a lookout for attacks.

Hadrian's wall

About 20 years later the Romans built a second wall between the Firth of Clyde and the Firth of Forth. It was made of blocks of soil with grassy roots called turf. The wall had forts and wooden battlements and was called the Antonine Wall, after the Roman Emperor of that time.

THE PICTS

The Romans gave a new name to the north, calling it the land of the Picts. "Pict" was a nickname for "painted people". The "paint" may have been blue dye used to paint warriors before battle, or, maybe they were tattooed. The "paint" may simply have described the colourful "tartans" worn by the tribes. Very little is known about the Picts because they left no written records other than a few mysterious "words" on carved stones. These beautiful carvings in stone show pictures of warriors, animals and strange beasts. It was thought that the power to rule, or to become a Pictish king, came from marrying a Pictish princess. The crown passed through the female side of the family, not the male side. Today, many historians disagree about this tradition.

The People Between The Walls

Three major tribes lived between the two Roman walls. The first were the Votadini, who were friendly to the Romans. They had three great strongholds: Traprain Law, Din Eidyn (Edinburgh) and Stirling which was north of the Antonine Wall. The second tribe called Novantae, lived in Galloway. Strathclyde was the home of the Damnonii, the third tribe. They established their capital in Dumbarton which was also north of the Antonine Wall. The Romans had divided the territories of these tribes with their new wall.

Pictish Carving

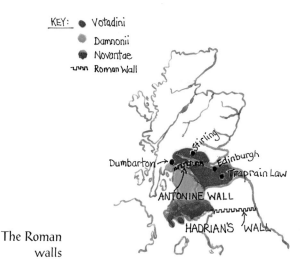

KEY:
● Votadini
● Damnonii
● Novantae
〜 Roman Wall

The Roman walls

The Picts continually attacked and raided the Antonine Wall and after only 20 years, the Romans gave it up and retreated to Hadrian's Wall. The attacks did not stop. In 209 AD the Romans marched into Pictland again but they still did not conquer the people or settle the land. By about 400 AD the Romans prepared to leave Britain. They left the north first.

THE FIRST SCOTS

At about the same time, people known as the Dal Riata, began to settle on the west coast around Kintyre. They were from Ireland where many of their families and their king remained for some time. Like the Picts they were descendants of the Iron Age Celts. Also like the Picts, they had a nickname, the "Scots", which meant "raiders." The language they spoke was an old form of Gaelic.

How They Lived

Life for the folk of Dal Riata, or Dalriada, was similar to that of other tribal groups. They lived in fortified settlements and round houses. Their king, or chief, was chosen by the heads of the families or clans. The wealthy farmers had cattle, sheep and pigs as well as oxen for drawing the plough. They planted crops and kept bees for honey.

They were also fishermen. Their boats, called curraghs, were made with a covering of hides painted with pitch (tar).

They had tools of iron, such as knives, saws and axes. There were rakes and sickles for gathering crops. The women ground grain to make bread and they also made butter, cheese and ale. Simple cups and buckets were made of wood and iron. Rich folk made candles from animal fats and the poorer folk used rush lights (oil lamps with wicks made from bulrushes).

Laws and Customs

People lived according to the laws and customs of the tribe. These laws were not written down and there were no courts or judges. If a person broke the law then the injured person's family took revenge or claimed payment in some form, often cattle.

Dalriada

THE ANGLES

When the Roman soldiers left the south, the Britons were open to attack from people searching for land. Angles and Saxons from Scandinavia and Germany crossed the north sea to take up land and to settle. Britons were pushed into Wales, Cornwall and north into Strathclyde. By 550, the Angles had moved north and established a kingdom first in Yorkshire and then finally extending as far as the River Forth. They were strong enough to hold the land against the Votadini and from attacks by the Strathclyde Britons. Even the Picts and the Scots could not push them back. The Angles called their kingdom Bernicia, later known as Northumbria. The language they spoke was an old form of English.

How they Lived

The Angle warriors carried round wooden shields. The men wore linen trousers strapped to the leg with cloth strips. Over this they wore a short woollen tunic. They wore leather shoes. Women wore long tunics of wool or linen.

The Angles built small oblong houses in villages protected by high wooden walls. These villages were called "tuns". They farmed the land in strips with everybody having a share of good land and poorer land. They shared a common grazing pasture. A very rich man might have his own "tun" with a great hall where he could entertain guests with feasting and music.

The Angles

Laws and Customs

The Angles made laws. When crimes were committed the nobles and freemen held meetings to decide upon a person's guilt. A guilty person had to pay compensation to the family he had wronged. Sometimes guilty men were made outlaws and could be killed if they came back to the village.

The Scots Grow Stronger

While the Angles gained strength and took more land, Fergus Mor, King of the Scots, decided to leave Ireland forever. He made the settlement of Kintyre his new kingdom in about the year 500. Like the Angles, the Scots wanted more land and Fergus Mor fought both the Britons of Strathclyde and the Picts for greater territory.

CHRISTIANITY

The Celtic people probably heard about the new faith from Christian Romans but the first missionaries, or preachers, were St Ninian and St Columba.

In 563 St Columba arrived in Dalriada. He was from a royal family in Ireland and although he was a monk he was also a warrior. He came to the island of Iona after a great battle and decided to set up a monastery with his 12 companions. Columba travelled throughout Dalriada teaching the Christian faith. He helped to unite the people under the leadership of one king, Aedan, great grandson of Fergus Mor. Columba also travelled into the land of the Picts and visited Brude, King of the Northern Picts, near Inverness.

St Columba

The monks built monasteries and taught young boys how to read and write. Some of these boys became monks when they grew up. Women who took up a religious life became known as nuns. Aiden, a monk from Iona, converted the Angles to Christianity. He set up the monastery at Lindisfarne in 635.

Laws and Customs of Christianity

In time, the beliefs and customs of the Christain faith had a great influence over the people. It was a "way of life" that was outside the laws and customs of the tribe. Gradually the different tribes who became Christian had religion and the laws of the church to bind them together.

Iona

The Battle of Nectansmere

By 638 the Angles had captured Dunedin (Edinburgh) and Stirling and in 685 they crossed the Forth into Pictland led by their king, Ecgfrith. They wanted to conquer the Picts who gathered under the leadership of their king, Brude. The Battle of Nectansmere was very important. The Picts defeated the Angles, defending the Highlands from the Lowlanders. After this, the Angles mostly remained south of the Forth where the Lowland language became English.

THE NORSEMEN

In Orkney, Shetland and around the coast of Caithness, Norn was the language spoken. It was the language of the early Norse settlers who left Scandinavia in search of land and a better life. The lands claimed by the Norse settlers included the Hebrides and the Western Isles and were ruled by powerful earls for the King of Norway.

These early Norse settlers were farmers and fishermen. They built strong oblong houses with stone walls. These were packed with earth and turf to keep out the wind. Turf covered the roof. Inside were two rooms, one for the family and the other a byre where the animals sheltered during winter. This style of house eventually became common across the land. The farmers used simple wooden ploughs and grew small crops of corn. They kept sheep and cattle. The Norse settlers married local people and followed the Christian faith.

THE VIKINGS

Later on, in the 8th Century, other Norsemen who were raiders and pirates arrived. They were known as the Vikings. For over 100 years the Viking raiders plundered the islands and coastlines of Pictland, Dalriada, Ireland and England. They killed or captured the people, burnt their homes and churches, stole their silver and gold and cattle. People lived in fear day and night. There was little they could do to protect themselves.

Iona Attacked

In 795 the Vikings attacked Iona. It was the first of many attacks. In a raid in the year 806, 68 people were killed on Iona. Some treasures had been saved and were moved to safe places. The book of Gospels with its beautiful drawings called illuminations, was moved to Kells in Ireland. Other sacred things were taken inland to Dunkeld, which became the religious centre for the country though kings were buried on Iona for many years after this.

At this time the various regions of the country were ruled by a number of kings or chiefs. None of them was strong enough to repel the Vikings.

Iona attacked

THE FIRST KINGS
KENNETH MACALPIN – KING OF ALBA

In 841 Kenneth MacAlpin, a descendant of Fergus Mor, became King of the Scots in Dalriada. He was a great warrior and fought anyone who would not accept his rule. He

tried to protect his people from the Viking raiders and soon he had a strong army. In 843 he took his army into Pictland.

The Picts were tired of fighting the Vikings and they knew Kenneth MacAlpin was a strong leader. Because of his Pictish mother Kenneth had a right to be their king. In the past, many Picts had married Scots and they were mostly simple Christian folk living off the land. They were happy to have a powerful king. So Kenneth MacAlpin was now king of two lands, Scotia, or Dalriada, and Pictland.

The lands were known as Alba in the Gaelic tongue. Kenneth MacAlpin was king of Alba for 16 years. He defended his country from the Angles of Bernicia who again tried to move north of the Firth of Forth. He also fought the Britons of Strathclyde as well as the Vikings. He died in 859 and was buried on Iona.

The Stone of Destiny – Making Scotland's Kings

The main centre for the kings of Alba was moved to Scone, near Perth, a sacred site for the Picts. Here kings were made at a ceremony while seated on a stone. The stone became known as "The Stone of Destiny". In those times the crown did not pass from father to son. Kings were chosen by the royal family and very often they reached the throne after plotting against each other or even killing their opponents. There were 13 kings between 859 and 1005 and 7 of them had been killed in blood feuds or by their successors. Malcolm II reached the throne by murdering Kenneth III in 1005.

The making of a king

MALCOLM II AND MACBETH

Malcolm II was a strong king and soon decided to claim the lands of Bernicia for Alba. In 1018 he conquered the Angles at the battle of Carham with the help of the Strathclyde Britons. Shortly afterwards, the Strathclyde king, Owen the Bald, died. Malcolm made his own grandson, Duncan, the Strathclyde king. Strathclyde was now part of Scotia.

One land, Scotland

Malcolm II, who was a descendant of Kenneth MacAlpin, brought together all the people and lands which now make up Scotland. By this time the old Roman nickname "Picts" had disappeared and all the various tribes gradually became known as Scots. Although the way of life, customs, styles of dress and housing in each part of the land differed, a new nation, led by one king, had come into being.

Malcolm died in 1034 and his grandson Duncan became king. Unfortunately the Northern Scots did not agree, claiming Macbeth should be king. This argument was settled in a battle in 1040 when Duncan was defeated and killed. Macbeth became King of Scotland and ruled for 17 years.

Then Duncan's son, also named Malcolm, marched against Macbeth with the help of the English king, Edward the Confessor. After several years of fighting Macbeth was slain. Malcolm then killed all of Macbeth's family to make sure that his own sons would inherit the crown. The system of choosing the best man for king was ended.

MALCOLM III

Malcolm III became King of Scotland in 1057 and members of his family ruled for the next 200 years.

The Norman Invasion of England

The year 1066 is one of the most important dates in British history. In that year, William the Conqueror invaded England with his Norman knights and won the great Battle of Hastings. With the help of his knights, he took control of England and built many castles across the country. Soon the Normans became more powerful than most of the English nobles.

St Margaret – Queen of Scotland

One person who escaped from the Normans was a Saxon princess, Margaret. She reached the Firth of Forth by boat and went to King Malcolm at Dunfermline, where he kept his

Queen Margaret

court. Margaret and Malcolm were married in 1070.

The new queen brought many improvements as well as English customs to the Scottish court. Instead of ale, wine was served at meals. She introduced spiced meats which were served on plates of gold and silver, and she made the royal palaces more comfortable and beautiful. Soon the court spoke English, rather than Gaelic.

Margaret worked hard to help the poor and needy and started the building of Dunfermline Abbey. The Queen also established a ferry service across the Forth. The Queen's Ferry was for people making the journey to St Andrews which was now the most important church in Scotland. People who travelled to holy places were called pilgrims. The towns of North and South Queensferry became busy and important places.

Both King Malcolm and Queen Margaret died in 1093 and were buried in Dunfermline Abbey. Because of the life she led, the Queen was called Saint Margaret after she died. Dunfermline Abbey became a place for pilgrims to visit.

Queen Margaret's Sons

After Malcolm's death there were rebellions. The Celtic people of the north did not want the "English" ways. Three of Margaret's sons ruled Scotland over the following 50 years: Edgar from 1097 to 1107, Alexander I from 1107 to 1124, and David I from 1124 to 1153.

THE NORMANS IN SCOTLAND

Queen Margaret's sons knew that the Norman knights helped to make the English king strong and powerful. So they invited the Normans into Scotland. In return, the Norman lords were given land. Edgar made Edinburgh the principal town of the kingdom. He built many castles, especially in Strathclyde and Galloway. From these wooden fortress castles the Norman knights kept the peace for the Scottish king.

The Norman lords also brought their skilled artisans and officers who lived in the new castles. There were clerks to keep the records and bailies to keep the law. Foresters, falconers, tailors and taverners each had special skills. As time went by, men who worked at these trades used the names of the trades as "surnames".

A forester, a falconer and a tailor

Three Great Norman families

Many of the noble Norman families had a greater part to play in the future of Scotland. Robert de Brus was given land in Annandale. Bernard de Bailleul, who had estates in Yorkshire, was a friend of David I of Scotland. Others were given important posts or duties in government. Walter FitzAlan and all his heirs after him were called Lord High Stewarts of Scotland. Stewart is the Scots word for "Stewards". The Steward looked after all the taxes and money for the king. He could also take command of the king's army. This post was the most important in the kingdom. After a time the FitzAlan family used "Stewart" as their family name. Eventually the families of Bruce, Balliol and Stewart produced future kings of Scotland.

THE FEUDAL SYSTEM

Melrose Abbey

By the time David I was king, between 1124 and 1153, much of the Lowlands had been given to the Normans. They brought a new way of life to the southern part of Scotland. Towns grew up and the first great abbeys and monasteries were built.

The king, who wanted help from the Norman earls and barons, gave them parts of the land, or estates. The estates included the peasant folk who lived on the lands.

Knights

The Norman earls and barons became powerful and rich men who served their king as keepers of the law. They provided knights to help keep the peace and to fight in the king's wars. The knights wore chain mail and helmets with nose guards. They carried shields, spears and great swords. Each knight rode a war horse. The Norman men wore their hair cut short and they shaved off their beards. They looked very different from the ordinary folk of Scotland.

The Norman overlords gave some of their land to their knights. In return, the knights had to fight for their lord in times of war. They also helped to keep law and order.

The Normans arrive

The Peasant Farmer

The knights allowed the peasants to work the land in return for services and rent. The services might be to carry wood or to dig peat for the castle. The peasants had to help with the lord's ploughing and harvesting. The rent was mostly paid with eggs, sheep and pigs, as well as grain. In times of war the peasants had to march with the army as foot soldiers. This system of renting land for a fee, or feu, was called the Feudal System.

The Peasant House

The lowland peasant lived in a small farm toun or settlement which was protected by the lord and his knights. His house was usually of turf or wattle and daub (sticks and mud), with a thatched roof. The byre was at one end to shelter the cows and other farm animals in winter. The family shared the other end, sleeping on heather or straw beds. They had very little furniture. They used wooden cups and plates and spoons made of horn.

Farming

The peasants had strips, or rigs, of farmland outside the toun for growing crops. They grew oats and bere (barley) to make ale. The men shared the heavy work of ploughing. Each man brought his ox to make up the team. The great wooden plough needed eight oxen and a team of four men to pull it up the rigs. They ploughed one rig for each farmer and then ploughed a second and so on. This was fair as they could all plant their seed at the same time.

All the toun's folk helped in the harvest. The grain was taken to the lord's miller who was paid to grind it. The farmer also had to pay a tax to the lord for his grain. The women made butter, cheese and ale. They spun wool and linen from which they made cloth for simple clothes. They had to live on what they could grow and make for themselves.

At festival times the toun's folk enjoyed singing and dancing. Their sports included wrestling and football.

THE NEW BURGHS

New trading towns called burghs, developed. They were built at the feet of royal castles or at the mouths of great rivers where ships could dock. The king invited foreign merchants or "burgesses" to set up business in the new burghs. They paid taxes and custom duties to the king who granted the burgesses many rights. They could hold markets and collect a "toll" or fee from the peasants entering the burgh to sell their goods. They could hold annual fairs.

Burghs were protected by the king and were not part of the Feudal System. They did not pay feudal dues to an overlord and they did not have to perform any service.

Law and Order in the Burghs

The burgesses elected bailies to keep the laws. The bailies held law courts to punish criminals. Punishments included fines. Serious criminals were punished by floggings, branding or banishment. Cases which might end with the death sentence went to the Sheriff's Court. The Sheriff was a judge chosen by the king.

Trade

The burgesses traded with other countries selling wool, hides and furs as well as coal. They brought back luxurious things such as spices and silk. They lived in houses built along a High Street. Usually they had a garden, a shop called a booth, and a barn. The burgesses could not live from trade alone, so they kept a few cows and chickens and farmed strips of the town's land outside the gates.

Guilds

The first burgesses came from England, Denmark, Normandy and Flanders. New burgesses had to belong to a merchant's guild or a craftsmen's guild. The guilds collected money from their members and looked after any members who were sick, as well as widows and orphans.

Boys who wanted to become members of these guilds had to be apprentices for several years while they learned the trade. They lived with their master but received no wages. Once they passed a test they could set up their own business if they had enough money. If they did not, they became journeymen and were paid for their work.

THE CHURCH

The king also granted land and people to the Church. The bishops and abbots were usually men from noble families. They built monasteries where monks lived, worked and prayed.

The churchmen were well educated and kept in touch with their brothers in other countries. They were keen to learn new methods of farming. They raised great flocks of sheep for wool. They ran coal mines, quarries and lead mines where the poorest peasants worked. Soon the Church became very rich and powerful.

A bishop

The nobles built small churches for the ordinary folk. They chose the priest and gave him some land so he could look after himself. An area ruled by a bishop was called a diocese. In each diocese there was a cathedral, a great church, in the main town of the area. The most important bishop lived in St Andrews.

Apart from bishops, priests, abbots and monks there were different orders, or groups of friars. They were often known by the colours of their plain woollen robes; Black Friars, Grey Friars, and White Friars. They wandered the countryside preaching and also looked after the sick and the poor.

THE NOBILITY

Life for the wealthy nobles, the earls and barons, was far more comfortable than for the peasants. Gradually, buildings of stone replaced the first wooden fortresses.

Castles

Some of the greatest nobles lived in castles. It took many people to run the castle and they also lived inside the castle walls with their families. Inside the courtyard were stables for horses. There were byres for the cows which kept the castle supplied with milk, butter and cheese. There were workshops for carpenters and blacksmiths where tools and weapons were made. Dogs and falcons were kept for hunting.

Life in a Castle

The lord and his family lived in the main tower of the castle. They gathered in the great hall where guests were entertained. The family had private rooms as well. They stored clothes in large, wooden chests. Apart from beds, chairs and tables, there was little other furniture. Food was eaten from boards which were set up as tables at meal times. Only the lord and important guests sat on chairs on a raised platform. The rest of the household sat on stools or benches lower down in the hall. The family used knives and spoons as well as plates made of silver, pewter or wood. Other folk had to bring their own. There were no forks so everyone ate with their fingers. They ate meat, roasted or boiled, pies and fish. Sweetmeats were made from dried fruits, nuts and honey.

The family played chess, draughts and dice. They were entertained by minstrels and story-tellers. Stone seats were set into the walls by the narrow windows but there was no glass to keep out the wind and the rain. Instead there were wooden shutters. The stone floors were covered with rushes. Tapestries, large rugs stitched with pictures, hung from the stone walls. Fires were kept going most of the year because of the cold. Warm clothes were needed in these chilly castles.

HIGHLAND LIFE

Life in the far Highland glens did not change very much after the arrival of the Normans. The clans were cut off and protected by the rugged mountains and travel was difficult. The Highlanders spoke the Celtic language. They still wore the Celtic tartan and plaids woven from dyed wool.

Highland Farming

Families lived in small clachans, or groups of houses, sharing their cottages with their cattle in the winter. Each farmer had a share of the rigs, strips of land for growing crops, but the soil was poor. Ploughing was done by hand or with the help of a tough Highland pony. Sheep and cattle grazed on common land. When the sons of a family grew up, the farmer shared his land between them.

Farmers allowed "cottars" to build homes in the clachan and these folk helped work the land in return for a small patch of ground to grow their food. As time passed the farmer's land had to support more and more people.

Daily Life

The Highlanders sent their cattle to markets to sell for money. Otherwise they lived on oatmeal porridge and bannocks, milk, butter, cheese and eggs. There was fish from the rivers and lochs or the sea. They had hardy sheep for wool and meat. They ate chicken at weddings or festivals. Each house had a kail yard where green leafy kail, like cabbage, was grown. When there was no kail, the women cooked nettles.

Clan Life

The Highland way of life was based on the family or the clan. The clans controlled areas of the countryside. The people were loyal to the chief of the family. The clan chief was responsible for the safety of his people especially in times of hardship or famine. Farmers paid a rent to the chief's "tacksman" who looked after the land. The tacksman was also responsible for getting the clansmen ready for war. Clansmen followed their chief into battle out of loyalty. Great chiefs could raise large armies and so the king would try to win the support of these chiefs.

SHAPING THE NATION
DAVID I

King David I worked hard to bring a better way of life to the people of Scotland. He appointed judges to travel throughout the land to deal with the law. He organised a system of running the country with loyal men to help him. They had titles such as Chancellor, Chamberlain, Marshal and Steward. All the taxes collected and money that was spent had to be written down into books. A new system for weighing and measuring was introduced for the whole of Scotland. The first Scottish coins were made of silver. These things all helped to encourage trade.

The Red Lion

Making Scotland Larger

During the next 100 years Scotland's kings tried to make their kingdom larger. David and his grandsons, Malcolm IV and William I, fought against England because they wanted Northumbria, the land once called Bernicia. William I was known as "The Lion" because of the red lion on his yellow shield. This is the Lion Rampant – Scotland's emblem. William's son, Alexander II and his grandson, Alexander III wanted to win the Western Isles for Scotland. The Western Isles were ruled by the King of Norway.

ALEXANDER III

Alexander III was born in 1241. He was only eight when he was crowned king after his father's death. When he was ten, Alexander was married to the daughter of the English king, Henry III. There was peace between Scotland and England. By the time he was 20 years old, Alexander was able to rule on his own.

Winning the Western Isles

In 1263, King Haakon of Norway sailed a great fleet of longships to the west of Scotland. He wanted to show King Alexander he was still the ruler of the Western Isles. To prove

how strong he was he sent men and ships up Loch Long and then carried the ships across land to Loch Lomond. The rest of his fleet was caught in gales and three longships were washed onto the beach at Largs. When a large Scottish force appeared there was a battle on the beach. Haakon and his men returned to their ships. They visited the settlements and islands ruled by Norway. Many of the lords of the islands felt that Alexander III should be their king and Haakon realised the only way he would keep the isles was by warfare. Haakon became ill and died in Kirkwall. Three years later

Viking longships

Haakon's son sold the Western Isles to Scotland. To seal the peace, Alexander married his daughter to the new King of Norway. In 1283 they had a baby girl who was named Margaret.

Peace

Alexander had brought peace to Scotland. Trade developed and sea ships brought goods to the burghs which were growing bigger. The king had roads built between the royal burghs. On the land people made a living by growing crops and raising cattle or sheep as they always had done. But they were free from the fear of war.

The Maid of Norway

In 1286 Alexander died when he fell from his horse over the cliffs at Kinghorn in Fife. He had no sons and his three year old granddaughter, Margaret of Norway, was heir to the throne. The English king, Edward, was determined that Scotland and England would be united. He arranged a marriage treaty between his own son and Margaret of Norway. The Little Maid of Norway, Queen of Scotland set sail for Scotland. However, she became ill on the journey and died in Orkney.

Death of
Alexander III

SCOTLAND'S FIGHT FOR FREEDOM

The next period of Scotland's history is remembered as one of the most glorious. It is also one of the bloodiest. It was the first time that the ordinary people of Scotland banded together. They decided for themselves what they wanted for Scotland. It meant they had to fight and it meant they suffered greatly.

EDWARD I OF ENGLAND
Choosing a King

Edward I chooses
John Balliol

Thirteen powerful nobles claimed the right to be king but there were two main "competitors". Robert Bruce of Annandale and John Balliol both insisted they were the rightful heir to the throne. Both men had land in England as well as Scotland and each had an army of followers. To prevent a war, the Bishop of St Andrews asked the English King, Edward I, to help decide who should be king.

Edward Takes Control

Edward chose John Balliol. Old Robert Bruce passed his claim to the crown to his son, the Earl of Carrick, also named Robert Bruce.

Edward did not want a powerful king in Scotland. He wanted to control Scotland himself. For the next four years Edward ruled and John Balliol simply did as he was told. The people of Scotland became angry.

Alliance with France

In 1295 Edward ordered the Scots to help him fight the French. Scotland did not want to fight for England. Even John Balliol was against Edward's demand. He decided to join the French and fight the English. This was the start of a friendship with France which became known as the Auld Alliance.

Old Robert Bruce and other nobles who had land in England joined the English side. As a punishment, John Balliol took all the Bruce estates in Scotland and gave them to his own relative, John Comyn. He was the most powerful baron in the land. This caused great hatred between the Bruces and Comyns for years to come.

Edward, The Hammer of the Scots

King Edward was furious with Balliol. In 1296 he marched his armies into Scotland. They burned farmland and villages, killed and plundered. Edward destroyed Berwick-upon-Tweed, slaughtering men, women and children. He took many castles, including Edinburgh Castle. He captured King John and put him in prison in the Tower of London.

Edward marched as far as Elgin to teach the Scots a lesson. He took away the ancient Stone of Destiny used in the ceremonies to make Scotland's kings. He made the leading nobles and barons sign an Oath of Loyalty to the King of England. This was called the Ragman Roll because of all the seals and ribbons they stuck to it. Edward became known as "The Hammer of the Scots".

Edward I takes the Stone of Destiny to England

WALLACE

William Wallace was a landowner who refused to sign the Ragman Roll. He was made an outlaw and the English Sheriff of Clydesdale burned down his house and had William's wife put to death. In revenge, Wallace killed the sheriff and called the people to revolt against the English invaders. It was May 1297.

The Great Cause

Wallace took his band of fighters and moved across the country attacking the English as he went. Others took up the Great Cause. Andrew Murray gathered the Northern Scots of Moray. Few Scottish nobles offered support but the young Robert Bruce saw his chance of claiming the throne. He joined Wallace.

Wallace

At first Edward thought it would be easy to put down the revolt with his well-trained soldiers in armour. The Scots were mostly common folk with simple spears, axes, swords and daggers. They wore no armour. But the ragged army grew each day and more castles were being taken back from the English. After many months the men led by Wallace and those led by Murray met and together they marched to Stirling.

The Battle at Stirling Bridge

The well-trained, well-equipped English army headed north to meet the rebels in September 1297. With 300 cavalry and 10,000 foot soldiers and bowmen the English expected the Scots to surrender in fear.

But William Wallace and Andrew Murray had planned a trap. The ragged army was not afraid. Everyone waited, hidden in the woods, watching the heavy English horses, the chargers, approach the tiny wooden bridge which crossed the River Forth. Only half of them had crossed when the war cry, "A Wallace", was taken up as the Scottish warriors raced down to close the trap.

Battle of
Stirling Bridge

It was a bloody battle. The English were trapped by their own dead on Stirling Bridge. The others were trapped by the marshy ground. Their heavy armour stopped them from escaping. The English lost many men. Andrew Murray was wounded badly and died two months later but he and Wallace had proved victory was possible. If the people wanted it, Scotland could be free.

Guardian of Scotland

Wallace became Guardian of Scotland and he fought to have John Balliol, Scotland's King, returned to the throne. Many of the nobles were jealous of Wallace. Others would not serve under a common man. Wallace took raiding parties into England and then, in the winter, he won back Stirling Castle. He opened up the ports and encouraged trade with Germany.

Defeat at Falkirk

In the meantime Edward planned to crush the Scots. He gathered a vast army. He met the Scots at Falkirk in July 1298. Here, Wallace had to face the full force of the English on open ground. It was not the way he wanted to fight. All he had was the courage of his peasant army and they did not let Scotland down. The English charged in wave after wave over the tightly packed circles of brave Scots warriors. This time however, the great strength and weapons of the English won the battle. Wallace managed to escape.

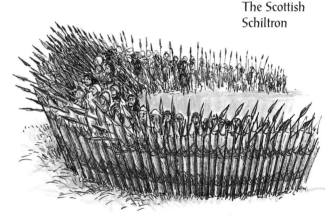

The Scottish Schiltron

Edward marched on and burnt St Andrews before returning south. However, the courage of Wallace and his peasant army inspired others to continue the fight for freedom. Edward had won a battle but, he had not defeated the people of Scotland.

Guerilla tactics

The Fight for Independence

After Falkirk, Wallace gave up the leadership of Scotland but for the next five years he and others led uprisings and attacks against the English. Wallace taught the Scots how small bands of fighters could fight large armies. This kind of fighting is called guerrilla warfare from a Spanish word *"guerra"* meaning little war. Edward invaded Scotland with huge armies six times during those years. He was unable to gain complete power over the Scots. These wars became known as the Wars of Independence.

In 1304 Edward planned to capture both Stirling Castle and William Wallace. It took Edward three months before he won Stirling Castle even though he had mighty war machines. These could bombard the walls and hurl great boulders and fireballs inside the castle. The small force, or garrison, holding the castle only surrendered because they had run out of food.

Wallace Betrayed

In 1305 Wallace was betrayed and captured. He was taken to London where he suffered the cruel death of a traitor. His body was cut up and sent to Newcastle, Berwick, Perth and Aberdeen as a warning to rebels. Wallace had remained loyal to the King of Scotland, John Balliol, and died bravely. He became a great hero to the Scottish people. He was a symbol of freedom.

Wallace execu[t]

Edward then decided to make peace with Scotland and he invited the Scots to help draw up the new laws in Parliament in 1305. He allowed the Scots to have their old laws and ways as they had under King Alexander III, but Edward was their king. There was no Scottish king.

ROBERT THE BRUCE
Robert Takes the Crown

Now Robert Bruce saw his chance to rule Scotland. He met with John Comyn, his rival for the throne, at the church in Dumfries on 10 February 1306. During an argument Comyn was stabbed and killed by Robert and his men. Robert had himself crowned King of Scotland on 25 March 1306 at Scone. He raised a band of followers and began to recapture castles and towns across Scotland. When Edward heard the news he vowed to capture Bruce and his followers and execute them as he had done Wallace.

Bruce crowned

Edward's Revenge

The Earl of Pembroke led Edward's English army but after a year Bruce had still not been captured. Edward of England ordered three of Robert's brothers to be executed. He imprisoned Robert's wife, his daughter Marjory and his two sisters.

Edward I

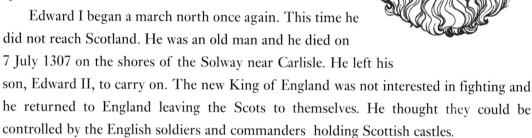

One sister was sent to a nunnery but the other was kept in a "cage" in Roxburgh castle. Edward had many of Bruce's supporters outlawed and hanged. The Countess of Buchan was harshly treated because she had helped Bruce to be crowned. She was kept in a "cage" in Berwick Castle for four years and only her English guards were allowed to speak to her.

Edward I began a march north once again. This time he did not reach Scotland. He was an old man and he died on 7 July 1307 on the shores of the Solway near Carlisle. He left his son, Edward II, to carry on. The new King of England was not interested in fighting and he returned to England leaving the Scots to themselves. He thought they could be controlled by the English soldiers and commanders holding Scottish castles.

Bruce Reclaims Scotland

Robert the Bruce now had to make sure his crown was safe. He led his army against the clans and followers of Balliol and Comyn, killing their families, destroying their strongholds and crops, and taking their livestock. This type of punishment was called "herschip". For two years Robert and his army marched across Scotland and into the Highlands, capturing castles and putting down rebels. Once he was in control of all the clans he planned to get rid of the English.

There were many castles and strongholds held by English soldiers but Robert did not win them all in battles or sieges. Like Wallace, Bruce and his men used guerrilla tactics, or tricks.

Taking Perth

Tricks and Tactics

To take the stronghold of Perth, Bruce led his men in the dead of night. He waded into the deep moat and led them up the walls using hooks and rope ladders. The stronghold was taken by surprise.

James Douglas and his men took Roxburgh Castle for Scotland. They wore black capes and crept up to the castle walls looking like black cattle in the darkness of night. They captured the castle easily.

Thomas Randolph planned to take Edinburgh Castle for Bruce. Some of his men attracted the attention of the

English at the gates of Edinburgh Castle while Thomas and his men were led up the steep rock face by a local man. Edinburgh Castle was taken for Bruce.

Bruce's men never faced the English in battle. Like the early Celts they made good use of Scotland's rugged mountains as hiding places. They travelled quickly on foot or on Highland ponies. Between 1308 to 1314, they raided the English supplies and won back the strongholds.

Taking Roxburgh Castle

Taking Edinburgh Castle

Stirling Castle

Stirling Castle, still held by the English, was under siege by Robert's brother, Sir Edward Bruce. He arranged with the commander of the castle to surrender if the English King had not rescued them by Midsummer. Neither Robert Bruce nor Edward II wanted a battle but they could not refuse. It was a challenge.

Edward II marched north with almost 3,000 cavalry, and more than 15,000 foot soldiers and bowmen.

Bannockburn

On Sunday 23 June 1314, the Battle of Bannockburn started. Like Wallace before him, Robert had planned traps. His men were hidden in the woods and on the high ground. He had dug pits. He planned to make the marshy land work against the English in their heavy armour. His men were strong and ready to fight.

Battle of Bannockburn

Only the Balliols, the Comyns and the Earl of Athol refused to stand with him. The rest of Scotland stood with their King against the English.

By sunset the English had attacked three times and three times they had been driven back. Only 6,000 Scots faced Edward. He thought he could not be defeated by such a small band of men. He moved his men down to the banks of the marshy burn where they could get water during the night.

The following morning Robert Bruce led his men down the hill. When the English cavalry came forward to meet them the Scots pushed them back into the marsh. The English spearsmen and bowmen were trapped by their own knights and heavy horses. The Scots advanced again.

No matter how bravely the English fought they had little chance and finally the men at the back began to run for their lives. The King of England escaped to his ships in Dunbar. Many of the English drowned in the Forth.

The Declaration of Arbroath

After Bannockburn, Robert punished the Balliols, Comyns and the Earl of Athol by taking away their lands. He had other problems as well. Edward refused to accept defeat and continued the war with Scotland.

Because he had killed John Comyn in a church, Robert was excommunicated, that is, cut off and not recognised by the church and the Pope. This meant that other countries would not recognise him as a king either. Robert called a council to write a letter which became one of the most important documents in Scottish history, the Declaration of Arbroath.

In 1320 the Declaration of Arbroath was drawn up and sealed by 8 earls and 31 barons. It was a letter to the Pope explaining that the Scots were a free people who wanted to live in peace. They asked the Pope to tell Edward of England to stop the wars. They said they would choose another king to fight for Scotland's freedom if Robert Bruce did not defend his country. It was the duty of the king to protect his people and that is what Robert Bruce had done.

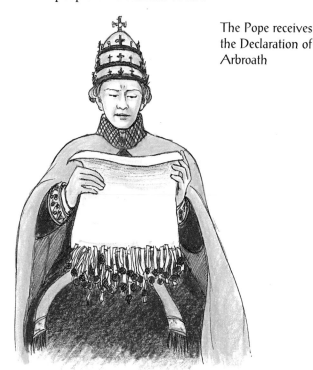

The Pope receives the Declaration of Arbroath

"For so long as one hundred men remain alive, we shall never under any conditions submit to the rule of the English. It is not for glory, or riches, or honours that we fight, but for freedom alone, which no good man gives up but with his life."

Robert was finally recognised as king, and at last, Scotland was independent. Wallace had not died in vain. There was a truce between Scotland and England. People hoped for peace.

Scotland After Bannockburn

For over 40 years the people of Scotland had suffered from the wars. Castles and other strongholds were left in ruins. Whole towns had been burnt. Churches had been robbed and spoiled. Thousands of people had been killed with great cruelty. It left Scotland poor.

The Land

Those who suffered most were the folk on the land – the peasants who thought freedom was more important than life and land. With the men away fighting, the work on the land was done by the women, children and the old folk. Very few crops were harvested. If the English did not burn them then the people themselves set fire to the fields. They would not let the English have their food. They kept just a few animals which they could take away to safety if necessary. It was a hard way to live.

The Burghs

The burghs suffered too. Trade with other countries stopped because there were no goods to send abroad. Other countries did not want to send ships into a country at war in case they were attacked. The peasants had little to sell and no money to buy goods either.

Bruce's Parliament

Robert was a wise ruler. In 1326 he invited men from the burghs for the first time to join his parliament along with those from the church and the nobility. They swore an oath of loyalty to Robert's baby son, David. They agreed to pay taxes in order to run the government. Robert built a navy to protect Scottish ships from English pirates. He wanted to repair the damages of war.

Death of Robert the Bruce

In 1329 Robert Bruce died. He was buried in Dunfermline Abbey. Bruce's heart was put in a silver casket to be taken on a crusade by James Douglas. The heart was buried in Melrose Abbey. In 1998 Bruce's heart was reburied in a new lead cannister.

The Melrose
Heart Casket

DAVID II
The Young King's Regents

Bruce's son was only a child and too young to rule the country. Regents, or guardians, were chosen to rule for him until he was old enough to take on the responsibility. They also educated the young king and protected him.

A child on the throne was a dangerous situation for the country. Scotland would have six more children on the throne in the next few 100 years. Sometimes regents were good and loyal. Often they were greedy, powerful people who thought more of themselves than their country. There was usually unrest and trouble as other powerful nobles and clan chiefs fought and quarrelled with each other. They tried to get control over the government.

The child King

Scotland's new king, David II was only five years old. By the time he was eight, both his loyal guardians were dead.

England Plots to take David's Throne

England's new king, young Edward III saw a chance to take the crown of Scotland. In 1332 he sent Edward Balliol, son of John Balliol to claim the Scottish throne. The Scottish lords sent David II to France for safety. War returned to Scotland. John Randolph, Andrew Murray and Robert the Steward tried to push Balliol and the English out of the country.

It took 11 years before Scotland was made safe enough to call David II back from France in 1341.

King David

David began to repair some of the great damage done to the land. Law and order were restored and folk returned to their lives as farmers and craftsmen. The burnt towns such as Haddington and Linlithgow were rebuilt.

Tower Houses

After the Wars of Independence, many of the nobles had replaced their damaged castles with tower houses. These were strong fortresses which would keep their families safe in case of another war. Tower houses had storerooms on the ground floor. Above that was the main hall or living area and above that were private rooms with attics at the very top. With one winding staircase, it was easy to defend against intruders.

Tower houses were often built on high ground to give a good view of the surrounding lands. There were small buildings outside and some houses had gardens for growing fruit and vegetables. Such houses protected the noble's family but they were not important or big enough to be useful to an enemy.

The Auld Alliance

In 1346 the French called on Scotland and the Auld Alliance to help them against Edward III of England who had invaded France. David raised an army and planned to fight his way to London. He thought it would be easy to take the city when Edward was in France.

David Captured

At Neville's Cross near Durham, the Scottish army met with a large English army. David made many mistakes in the battle of Neville's Cross. Scotland lost many of her most powerful nobles and David II was captured and taken to the Tower of London as a prisoner.

Robert the Steward

David remained King, but Robert the Steward was appointed the Guardian of Scotland. During the following years, people tried to lead a normal life again. However, Balliol raised a small army and took back all the lands he had lost before 1341. He gave these lands to Edward of England. It seemed as if Scotland would never be free. Only the castles of Stirling, Dunbar and Edinburgh held out and remained under the control of King David and Robert the Steward.

King David captured

The Black Death

In 1349 another great tragedy hit the folk of Scotland. This was the Black Death, the plague. The plague was a deadly disease caused by the fleas from rats and it started with sneezing. The illness attacked people's bodies with boils and black swellings. Most people died in great pain after only a few days. So many people died that the bodies had to be thrown onto carts and buried in great pits.

For two years the plague raged, mostly among the poor folk. Many of the rich were safe because they lived in stone houses away from the crowded, dirty townships. The plague returned from time to time over the next centuries.

A Ransom for David

By 1352 Edward of England needed money for his wars in France. He had thought of a new way to get the throne of Scotland as well. He offered to release David II for a ransom and a promise. He wanted the money but he also wanted the Scots to promise that he would become the Scottish king if David did not have an heir. The Scottish lords refused. They would never have an English king

Balliol Gives Up

By this time, Balliol knew he would never be accepted by the Scots. Even worse, his loyalty to Edward of England had made him poor. In 1356 Balliol handed his crown to Edward and gave up his claim to the kingship of Scotland.

Edward receives Balliol's crown

Edward Marches into Scotland

Since he now had this crown, Edward felt he had the right to take Scotland by force. However, as he marched up through the borders he found the land had been stripped bare. The people had burned their own crops and moved all the livestock away. There was nothing for the English army to take. In revenge Edward destroyed churches and holy shrines.

When the English reached Edinburgh they hoped for supplies which were coming by sea. But great storms kept the ships away and Edward had to return to England.

David Returns to Scotland

The situation was not good for either England or Scotland. Years of war and plague had made both countries poor and the hardships suffered by the people had to end. Robert the Steward, Scotland's guardian, arranged for the return of David II with a vast ransom which was to be paid to England each year for ten years.

David returned to Scotland in 1357. He reigned as king for 14 years before his death in 1371. During this time, peace, law and order returned and life was safer for the people.

THE ROYAL HOUSE OF STEWART

David II died without a son to take the throne. Instead, the crown of Scotland went to Robert the Steward. His mother was Marjory, daughter of Robert the Bruce. Robert II was 55. He had twice been the Guardian of Scotland. His reign began the Royal House of Stewart and for the next 300 years, Scotland was ruled by his heirs.

ROBERT II
The Border Barons

Robert II ruled peacefully for some years. However, many of the nobles preferred fighting to peace. In the Borders especially there were powerful barons who lived in great stone castles. They raised armies to fight for the king and Scotland but if there was no war they had to find other ways to keep their men and castles. Some barons made money by hiring out their armies to fight for kings in Europe. Others sent their armies across the border to raid and plunder the lands of English nobles. These barons were strong and wealthy and they were a threat to the king.

Robert II

Border reivers

When the truce between England and Scotland ended in 1384, the nobles prepared for war with England. The Auld Alliance was still in place and the French were happy to send both money and men to help Scotland fight the English. They wanted to make England weak.

Scotland herself was weakened by all the strife. Once more crops were burned. Men made a living as part of raiding parties instead of farming. Trade suffered and pirates ruled the seas. When Robert II died his son became king in 1390.

ROBERT III

The new king, Robert III, was no stronger than his father had been. He could not control the warlords. When his young son David, the next heir to the throne, died, Robert thought he had been murdered. Robert wanted to keep his younger son, 12 year old James, safe. He planned to send the prince to France.

Prince James sailed from Leith on 14 March 1406, but he was captured by English pirates and sent to the Tower of London. When King Robert heard the news he was already a very sick man. The news of his son's capture caused him such pain that he died on 4 April 1406.

JAMES I
Prince and Prisoner

The young prince became King James I of Scotland while he was held by the English. He was not an ordinary prisoner. James had tutors who taught him music, languages, writing and, of course, the skills of a warrior.

Albany in Power

In the meantime his country was ruled by the Duke of Albany, the regent. Albany did very little to gain the release of James and ruled as if he was the king.

Scotland had a fairly peaceful time. Trade developed and Scotland's first university was established at St Andrews in 1412. When the Duke of Albany died, his son Murdoch became the new regent in 1420. During this time the barons became more powerful.

James I Returns

In April 1424 James I and his queen, Joan, crossed the borders to take control of the country. James was a young man but he was not afraid of the barons or the nobles who were bringing misery to the people.

Restoring Law and Order

James began restoring law and order even before he was crowned at Scone on 21 May. Murdoch, Duke of Albany, was tried and executed for treason.

The young king used parliament to make laws which dealt with many problems. Inns were built in the burghs and on the highways so that poor farmers did not have to give free food and shelter to travelling noblemen. Inside the burghs there were rules to help prevent fires and fire-fighting services were established. Landowners were not allowed to evict their peasants unless the land was needed by the lord. They also had to grow wheat, peas and beans besides the usual crops to provide a better diet.

Conservation

James was also interested in protecting the countryside. Many of Scotland's forests had been cut down so it became a crime to steal timber or peel bark from trees. Fishing nets used in fresh waters had to have holes big enough to let the young fish through. There were times when wildfowl could not be caught so they could nest.

Football Fines

James tried to organise the way people lived so that time was well used and money was not wasted. There were laws to prevent people from wearing costly clothes. Drinking ale in taverns after 9 pm was not allowed. He tried to put a stop to football by fining players four pennies. James thought they should be practising archery which would be useful in war time.

Keeping the Peace

James created law officers to make sure that peace was kept. Men were not allowed to raise private armies. By the end of his reign James had reduced the number of earls from 15 to

James confronts the clan chiefs

only 8. He held a special parliament at Inverness and called in all the clan chiefs. There had been a great deal of trouble in the Highlands between the clans. Most of the chiefs were imprisoned for a short time to teach them a lesson. Three chiefs were hanged. James insisted that the clan chiefs make peace and live under the law but it was almost impossible to stop the feuding.

The Death of James I

Because James was a strong king he made enemies among some of the nobles who had been punished by him. One of these enemies was Sir Robert Graham. He led a band of men into the Blackfriars Monastery at Perth on the night of 20 February 1437.

The king and queen were in their bedroom when they heard men in armour coming. James hid under the floorboards while the queen and her ladies tried to stop the men getting in. Graham and his men wounded the queen and butchered the king.

Queen Joan had the assassins hunted down. She took revenge by having the men tortured before being executed.

JAMES II
Twelve Years of Strife

Scotland was ruled again by a regent because the new king, James II, was only 6 years old. The nobles and clan chiefs fought amongst themselves for power and control over the throne. Lawlessness returned and the poor suffered from famine and plague. In 1439 the plague killed the regent. The keepers of Edinburgh and Stirling Castles fought to have control over the young King James.

James II on the Throne

The strife continued until James II was 18 years old. In 1449 James married Mary of Gueldres and took control of his war torn country.

James had grown up in fear for his life. He had witnessed the cruelty with which the regents had kept themselves in power. When he was a child, he saw two Douglas boys murdered by the Regent William Crichton after dinner at Edinburgh Castle. He feared he would be murdered one day, and so James knew he had to be stronger than his nobles.

The murder of Douglas

James Murders the Earl of Douglas

William, Earl of Douglas, the most powerful noble in the country, was plotting with other nobles against James. James decided to give him a chance to give up the plot and to swear loyalty to the king. William refused to give up his alliance with these nobles. James was in such a fury that he stabbed the Earl of Douglas to death. James decided it would a lesson to other rebels.

Within six years James had brought peace to the country. People were protected by the law. Glasgow University was founded in 1451.

James II Dies

In 1460 James decided to remove the English from the last stronghold in Scotland which was Roxburgh Castle. By this· time gunpowder and cannons were used in warfare. On 3 August, the Scottish cannon were ready to begin firing. James stood by a great cannon called "The Lion". He was killed when the cannon exploded. The Scottish army fought on for their dead king and after five days the English were finally driven out of Scotland.

James II and The Lion

JAMES III

Yet again a child king was crowned. James III was only eight. Peace was kept for several years because James's mother, Queen Mary, and Bishop Kennedy were good guardians. By the time James was 14 both his guardians had died.

James was kidnapped by a party of nobles led by Lord Boyd who became the king's guardian. He arranged for James to marry Margaret of Denmark. Because of this marriage, Orkney and Shetland became part of Scotland.

A Treaty with England

James III was a very different king from his father and grandfather. He hated warfare and the sports of the warrior such as fencing, shooting, hunting and jousting. For 18 years he tried to rule his kingdom and to maintain peace, law and order. However he could not win the loyalty of his nobles and discovered a plot between the Earl of Douglas and John, Lord of the Isles. James made a treaty with the English King Edward IV to protect himself against the rebel nobles.

James Murdered

In the end a battle was the only way to put down the rebel nobles. James's own son was on the side of the rebels. The battle was fought on 11 June 1488, close to Bannockburn and lasted until dark. Towards the end of the day James left the field on horseback. No one knows why he fled, but James was thrown from the horse and lay injured until a miller and his wife carried him to their cottage. James asked for a priest. Whoever came to him was an assassin. James was stabbed in the heart leaving his 16 year old son to be crowned at Scone on 26 June 1488.

James III assassinated

JAMES IV

Even though James IV was so young he was able to take control of the country and the government. He wanted no more bloodshed and since he was willing to talk to his nobles he gained their trust and their loyalty. It was time to establish peace in the land.

Life on the Land

James IV

Life on the land had not changed for hundreds of years. Landlords would only rent the land for a few years at a time. This meant the farmer could be evicted, told to leave his house and land. Because of this, most farmers did not waste time building better homes. Because of the poor methods of farming, there was usually only just enough to live on. Occasionally there was extra grain to sell. When winter started there was no feed left for cattle. Most of the cattle had to be slaughtered and salted to preserve for eating during winter.

The Burghs

The burghs had become much bigger townships over the years. The wooden houses were taller and there were more of them. Living conditions were unhealthy in the cramped spaces. The townsfolk still piled up the garbage and filth from their homes and their animals into the streets. There was plague and disease. The tightly packed wooden houses separated only by narrow dark wynds were always likely to catch fire. The burgesses still farmed the land beyond the town wall.

There were more burghs as trade increased. The import of fine goods such as wine, silk, spices and other luxurious goods made life more pleasant for those who could afford it.

Life of the Nobility

The fortress homes of the nobles became more comfortable. As life became more peaceful the wealthy lords built walled courtyards and gardens. Furniture was sometimes imported from Europe and there were tables, chairs and wardrobe chests. Four poster beds were hung with curtains to keep out the draughts. Fine cloth was imported from Europe to make fashionable clothes.

Many of the bishops and abbots who came from wealthy families lived as richly as the nobles.

Transport

There were new roads between the larger burghs but they were not always the easiest way to travel in bad weather. They were really only rough tracks. Whenever possible goods were transported by ship. There were few roads into the heart of Scotland and most of the Highlands remained isolated.

Trade

With peace came a better way of life for most people. Instead of the men being away at war, work could be done. Trade developed.

James ordered a great fishing fleet to be built. The coastal burghs caught more fish and did more trade with Europe. The export of herring brought in great wealth. Besides herring and salmon, the ships carried wool and hides, cloth, salt and coal. James also had ready-made fleet of ships if ever there was another war.

The Renaissance

James lived in the time called the Renaissance. It was a time of new learning and he was interested in every aspect of Science and the Arts. James liked new inventions and he was also interested in new designs for buildings and towns. He also loved music and poetry. William Dunbar and Robert Henryson were two of the country's favourite poets at this time.

Education

James believed in education and encouraged it. There was an Education Act which made sure that the lairds would send their eldest sons to school to study Latin and Law. James

wanted these children, who would one day be the leaders of their communities, to understand the law.

In 1495 the third university in Scotland was founded in Aberdeen. It was the first university to study and teach Medicine. Later, in Edinburgh, the College of Surgeons was founded in 1506. This college was supplied with the bodies of criminals so the students could learn how the human body works. They also sold a new medicine – whisky!

Learning became easier for everyone after this time because of the printing press. The first printing press was set up in Edinburgh in 1507.

Controlling Powerful Families

James learned to speak Gaelic and visited the Highlands six times in the first few years of his reign. He gave land to Highlanders who were not part of the royal family. He did this to break down the power of the barons. In the Lowlands, James set up new courts to punish families who were feuding.

Henry VIII of England

In 1503 James married Margaret Tudor, daughter of King Henry VII of England. It was a very great wedding, planned to bring Scotland and England closer together. Margaret's brother became Henry VIII, King of England in 1509. From that time on, the old troubles began again.

James ordered the building of naval dockyards and a great warship which took two years to complete. It had 21 guns and it was Scotland's first "man-of-war". It was called after the queen, Margaret. Later came an even greater ship, the *Michael*, which was launched in 1511.

The Michael

Scotland at War

By 1513 Henry VIII was planning to conquer France. The French queen sent her ring and a message to James. She asked him to remember the Auld Alliance and to help her country against the English.

James was not sure about involving Scotland in a war but he did gather a great army and he ordered his fleet out to sea. Then he sent a warning to Henry VIII who was already in France.

Margaret Tudor

Henry VIII

Another Fight for Freedom

King Henry sent back a message to say that he owned Scotland. Henry said he would take James off the throne when he returned from France.

Again Scotland had to fight for her freedom. The Scottish army crossed into England on 22 August 1513. Because it was such a vast army laden down with guns and supplies, it moved slowly. The Scots took the Border castles as they went.

An English army, just as strong, gathered to face the Scottish invaders. James was ready to take his army back into Scotland – the way Bruce had done in the past. However, the English were determined to make the Scots stand. They sent a challenge and James agreed to wait until 9 September to face the Earl of Surrey.

Flodden

The Scots held a good position but their great cannons were very heavy and soon the lighter English guns put them out of action. Then James made a serious mistake. Instead of standing his ground and waiting for the English to come, he led a charge downhill to meet them.

The men were carrying the traditional, huge, heavy Scottish spears. These were designed to be used by men standing closer together forming a tight forest of spikes. They were too heavy. The Scots had to throw them down as they moved up and down slippery slopes while the English were able to use their shorter, lighter "bills", spears with axes.

Key: FLODDEN FIELD
THE BORDER

St. Andrews
Edinburgh
Forth
Clyde
Glasgow
Berwick
Upon Tweed
Coldstream
ENGLAND

Flodden field

The Scots drew their swords and fought bravely. That day James IV died with 10,000 Scots on Flodden field. With them died a great number of the ruling nobles and many families were almost wiped out.

JAMES V

On 21 September 1513, James V was crowned the new king of Scotland. He was not even two years old. Scotland could not rejoice. There had been too many deaths. Scotland had paid a high price for helping the French and protecting their freedom.

Fourteen Years of Fear

Jedburgh torched

The next 14 years were troubled ones for the boy king and for Scotland. The Scottish lords chose the Duke of Albany who arrived from France in 1515 to be Guardian of the Realm. He was an honest guardian but he was often away in France. In 1522 Henry VIII sent an English force across the borders. Farms and forests were burned. Kelso and Jedburgh were torched and plundered.

The King Kept Prisoner

Young James fell under the control of Archibald Douglas, Earl of Angus, who became Guardian of the Realm. He kept the young prince James a prisoner for over three years and gave all the important positions in the country to his own relatives.

The Douglases Punished

In 1528 when James was 16 he managed to escape Douglas. He reached Stirling. James intended to take control of his country and punish his enemies.

With a small army he attacked Archibald Douglas in Tantallon Castle near North Berwick. Douglas surrendered and James banned him and his family from Scotland. The Douglases went to England.

The Border Wars

Like so many kings before him, James had to restore law and order in the land. In the Borders, James had to control the great Border families, the Earls of Home and Bothwell, the Maxwells, Scotts and many more. These robber barons went about the Borders, both the Scottish side and the English side, raiding, stealing and terrorising the poor folk as they pleased.

James knew that if he did not stop these powerful clan chiefs and their men he would soon have Henry VIII crossing the border to seek revenge. There would be war with England. James threw many of these men into prison. A well-known border cattle thief, Johnnie Armstrong of Liddesdale, and many of his men were hanged, all from the same tree.

The Highlands and Islands

When the powerful Earl of Argyll, Campbell Clan Chief, died in 1529 the MacDonalds of Islay and the MacLeans raided Campbell lands in revenge. James made several visits to the area to restore calm. Later he travelled with a small fleet of armed ships up to Orkney and back down the west coast. He took a number of clan chiefs prisoner and demonstrated that the Highlanders had to respect the king's law.

The Poor Man's King

He gradually brought peace to the land. He was a real hero to the common people and James became known as the Poor Man's King. He even had a nickname, The Guidman o Ballengreich. James liked to dress in the clothes of a farmer and ride round the countryside to see that his poor folk were happy. People knew who he was and loved him all the more. James enjoyed the adventures and the freedom his "disguise" gave him.

The Guidman o Ballengreich

Mary of Guise

The French Marriages

In 1537 James went to France to marry Princess Madeleine. She brought to Scotland a rich dowry. A dowry is the money and jewels given to the bride's husband at the time of the wedding. However, Madeleine was not a strong girl and she died shortly after arriving in Scotland. James soon found another wife from France, Mary of Guise. She also brought a very rich dowry to Scotland.

Greedy James

Now there was peace in the land and taxes were collected again. The treasury began to fill up with money. James grew greedier and taxed the nobles heavily. He also became suspicious of plots against him and punished suspect nobles harshly. They began to fear and distrust James.

Henry VIII and the English Church

In England, King Henry VIII had become the head of the church, breaking away from the rule of the Pope in Rome. Henry took all the wealth of the monasteries and abbeys for himself. He made enemies of the Catholic countries which remained loyal to the Pope. These countries wanted a war with England and they wanted James and Scotland to join them.

Henry Attacks Scotland Again

Henry still felt he was the "overlord" of Scotland. In 1542 he asked James to come to York to discuss various matters. However, the king's advisors feared that Henry planned to capture James and would not let him go.

Henry took his revenge on Scotland by looting, burning and wasting the borders. Roxburgh and Kelso were once more burned down.

Pope Clement III

The Defeat at Solway Moss

James had no choice but to raise an army. The Scots, remembering Flodden, were not too keen to go into battle. The Scottish army marched to the Borders but some of the nobles would not agree to cross into England. James sent them away in disgrace. He and his army marched towards Solway. On the way the king became ill and he rested in Lochmaben Castle while Oliver Sinclair took over the leadership of the army.

On 24 November 1541, the sad Scottish army was met by a small English army at Solway Moss. Many Scots surrendered rather than lose their lives for a king they did not trust. Twelve hundred Scots were taken prisoner and many others simply made an escape. It was a disaster.

James arrives at Falkland Palace

The Death of James and Birth of a Queen

The news was taken to James who knew he had failed his people. He rode to Edinburgh and then to Linlithgow where the queen was about to have their child. James rode to Falkland Palace. He was ill and news of the birth of a daughter only made him sadder. James died on 14 December 1542.

THE REFORMATION

The story of Scotland, England and the rest of the world was changed by religion during this time. People began to think about the Church and religion and what it should mean.

Many felt that the Church needed to be improved or reformed. This period in history is called the Reformation.

In England, Henry VIII had broken away from the Catholic church and the Pope. He became the head of the Church of England and he expected all his people to give up the Catholic faith. In France there were many people who "protested" against the Catholic faith. But the French King remained loyal to the Pope in Rome and he expected his people to do the same. But it didn't matter what kings said. A large number of people made up their own minds about what church they wanted to belong to.

In Scotland there were many who wanted a new church. They did not like the the power held by bishops who had great wealth. The poor folk especially wanted a church which would help them. They could not understand the services in Latin and they wanted a simple way of praying.

MARY QUEEN OF SCOTS

Scotland now had a queen, a new-born baby called Mary. She was crowned in December 1542 when she was just a week old. Almost immediately Henry VIII saw a way to gain complete control over Scotland. He began arrangements for his son Edward to marry Mary as soon as she was 11. Henry promised peace in the Treaty of Greenwich.

Henry VIII Plans a Wedding for Mary

Cardinal Beaton

Henry VIII sent Archibald Douglas, Earl of Angus back to Scotland with James Hamilton, Earl of Arran. Hamilton was very interested in the new Protestant faith and he became the Guardian of the Realm.

Cardinal Beaton, Archbishop of St Andrews, realised that Henry was trying to gain control over Scotland. He advised the Scots to remember the Auld Alliance. He said that France and the Catholics were safer for Scotland than England and the Protestants. Henry had the Cardinal arrested and locked up.

Henry VIII thought he was in a strong position. Once Mary was married to

Mary crowned

his son he would have control over Scotland. Henry wanted Mary brought up in the English court. He wanted an end to the Auld Alliance and he wanted to put English soldiers into Scottish castles.

The Scots Refuse Henry's Plans

Henry's actions were just as Cardinal Beaton had predicted. Even the Protestant Scots were angry with Henry. They were not going to give up their freedom. The Cardinal managed to escape and he and the Queen Mother forced Hamilton, Henry's Guardian of the Realm, to join their side. The Scottish Parliament refused to agree to Henry's conditions and they ended the Greenwich Treaty.

Henry's Revenge

In May 1544 a great fleet of English ships entered the Firth of Forth. No one in Edinburgh expected an attack. Henry's revenge was terrible. The Earl of Hertford's powerful army burned Edinburgh, destroying Holyrood Palace. Men, women and children were butchered as Hertford's men marched to Stirling. They burned over 200 villages and towns. When they marched south, the army destroyed the Catholic abbeys of Kelso, Dryburgh, Melrose and Jedburgh.

The burning of
Edinburgh

Religious Strife in Scotland

The slaughter of the poor, the women and children, was so dreadful that it was easy to blame Scottish Protestants for what had happened. Henry and England were protestant so any Scots who were protestant were also to blame. In 1545 the English attacked again.

Cardinal Beaton and Mary's French mother, Mary of Guise, wanted to keep the old Catholic faith safe. They captured the leaders and preachers of the new faith. They had many of them burned at the stake. Many Scottish Protestants had no choice but to escape to England and Henry. Scotland was divided over religion.

Cardinal Beaton and George Wishart

In 1546 Cardinal Beaton arrested a Protestant preacher, George Wishart. Wishart was taken to St Andrews and after a trial he was strangled and burned at the stake. Beaton watched from the palace window. Those who admired Wishart's courage and his faith took revenge on Beaton.

Wishart burned

Beaton killed

Two months after the burning, Beaton was stabbed and killed. He was hung out of the same window from where he had watched Wishart die.

Beaton's Protestant attackers occupied the castle of St Andrew's and were trapped by the queen's Catholic army. During that year, 1547, Henry VIII died leaving a young son, Edward VI.

The Earl of Hertford was made Duke of Somerset and Protector of England. The Scottish Protestants hoped he would come to help them and those trapped in St Andrews. John Knox went to St Andrews to preach and to join the Protestants in the castle.

France and England come to the Rescue

It was the French who came and revenged the death of Cardinal Beaton. They took the castle and imprisoned the Protestants who were nobles. The others were captured and sent to be galley slaves, rowers chained to the seats of French ships. John Knox was one of these, serving almost two years.

The Protector of England offered to protect the Scots from the French and the Pope. This was the same Hertford who had killed the women and children of Edinburgh. He marched on Scotland with a strong army. The English navy sailed north. They were determined to win Mary for the English king and to make Scotland Protestant.

The Battle at Pinkie

Scotland's regent, Hamilton, met the English near Musselburgh at a place called Pinkie on 10 September 1547. The Scots fought bravely but the English hammered them with cannon-fire from the fleets of ships. The Scottish long spears proved little use against the English axes and muskets. The Protector smashed the Scots and went on killing long after the battle was over. He took Leith and plundered Holyrood Abbey. He then moved north and attacked Dundee. As the English returned south they left soldiers in all of the captured castles and fortresses.

A French Marriage for Mary

It was clear to the Scots that England was more interested in conquering Scotland rather than uniting the two countries through a royal marriage. They turned again to France and the Auld Alliance.

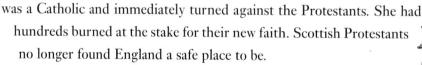

Mary leaves for France

France was interested in a marriage treaty with Scotland. They knew that Mary was an heir to the throne of England. If Mary married the French prince then one day France might rule England!

So the marriage was agreed. Five year old Mary Queen of Scots sailed off to the French Court in 1548. This was soon after the Battle of Pinkie. Mary's mother, Mary of Guise, ruled Scotland for her daughter with the help of French troops.

The English Throne

Mary Tudor

Elizabeth I

In England, Edward died, and his sister, Mary Tudor, became queen in 1553. She was a Catholic and immediately turned against the Protestants. She had hundreds burned at the stake for their new faith. Scottish Protestants no longer found England a safe place to be.

In France in 1558 Mary Queen of Scots married Francis the Dauphin. When the English Queen Mary Tudor died soon after, the Queen of Scots made a claim to the crown of England and Ireland. But Elizabeth I was crowned Queen in England and she was Protestant.

THE CHURCH OF SCOTLAND

The new Church of Scotland was growing stronger and more people felt the old church no longer served the poor and needy. While there were grand cathedrals for the rich towns and fine homes for the bishops, the churches for the poor often did not even have a priest. Priests were poorly paid and sometimes could not even read. The "protestors" demanded that the wealthy friars leave their houses and hospitals and give them back to the poor.

Religious Riots

John Knox returned to Scotland and after preaching against the Catholics there were riots. Churches and abbeys were wrecked.

Mary of Guise used French troops to control the uprisings of the new church. They marched from Edinburgh through Fife, Stirling and on to Glasgow.

Help for the new church came from the Protestant Queen Elizabeth of England. A fleet of ships arrived in the Firth of Forth in January 1560 and cut off the French supplies. The French troops returned to Leith. Soon they were trapped because an English army crossed the Borders and laid siege to Leith. Mary of Guise who was seriously ill was also at Leith and on 11 June she died.

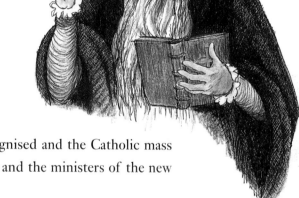

John Knox preaching

The Reformed Church of Scotland

The Treaty of Edinburgh restored peace and stated that the Auld Alliance should end. French troops had to leave Scotland. Both France and Scotland had to agree that Elizabeth I was the Queen of England.

By the end of 1560 the Church of Scotland had been reformed. The Pope was no longer recognised and the Catholic mass was forbidden. There were to be no more bishops and the ministers of the new "kirks" were to be chosen by the people.

Mary Returns to Scotland

On 19 August 1561, Mary Queen of Scots returned from France to take over the throne of Scotland. Mary's young husband had died and now Protestant Scotland had a Catholic queen. Though Mary promised not to interfere with the new Church of Scotland, the people were troubled. They did not want the old church to return and John Knox spoke out against Mary in the streets and kirks of Edinburgh.

Mary Takes Control

Mary chose Lord James Stewart and William Maitland of Lethington as her chief advisors. This was a wise choice because these men were Protestant. Mary also made sure that the new Church of Scotland received a share of the money from lands and properties of the old church.

Mary and the Highlanders

She then decided to travel about the country to meet the people. Her visit to the Highlands in 1562 was also a test of her strength as a ruler. There she had to put down an uprising of the Earl of Huntly and his sons. She won the hearts of her Highland lords because of her bravery.

Mary Marries Henry Darnley

On 29 July 1565, Mary married Henry Darnley who was a descendant of the Tudor King Henry VII. Before too long, however, Darnley was causing trouble and Mary had to make sure he had no royal powers.

Henry Darn

David Riccio

Mary had many advisors but one of her most trusted was a man called David Riccio, a Catholic and a foreigner. John Knox feared that Riccio was influencing the queen. Henry Darnley was jealous because the queen trusted Riccio more than himself.

On 9 March 1566, Darnley took a band of men led by the Earl of Ruthven into the queen's rooms where she was having supper with her friends. The Earl demanded that Riccio leave the rooms. When he would not, he was dragged out. Riccio was stabbed to death. Mary was very angry and very upset but she had to be careful. Darnley was dangerous and Ruthven and his followers frightened her.

Darnley's Death

In June Mary had her baby, a son to inherit the throne of Scotland. By this time Darnley had lost many friends because of his drinking and gambling. When he became ill the following winter, Mary had him brought to a small house called Kirk o' Field near the palace. She visited him several times there but on the night of 9 February the house blew up. Darnley and his servant were found dead outside the house. Darnley had been strangled.

The Earl of Bothwell

Earl of Bothwell What happened is still a mystery. It may have been a plot to kill Mary. Many people believed the queen with her friends planned the murder. One of her friends, James Hepburn, Earl of Bothwell, was to go on trial. Bothwell, however, was a powerful man and he brought his men into Edinburgh and the trial did not take place.

Three months later Mary married Bothwell. The people of Scotland were shocked. Many did not trust the queen. Rebellions broke out. Some people felt the queen was no longer important since there was a prince to wear the crown.

Bothwell was made an outlaw. He escaped to Denmark but the Danish King arrested him. Bothwell was chained inside a dungeon. He died years later, a madman.

Mary Gives Up the Throne

Mary Queen of Scots gave herself up to the Protestant lords on 15 June 1567. She was made a prisoner in the island castle of Loch Leven, Kinross. She had to give up her throne and allow her baby son to be crowned James VI of Scotland. Mary's half-brother, the Earl of Moray, was made regent.

Loch Leven
Castle

A Prisoner in England

Mary escaped from Loch Leven after almost a year. Her plans to regain the throne failed. She escaped to England but Elizabeth would not help her. Instead, Mary was kept a prisoner in England and was moved from one castle to another for almost 20 years.

She was heir to the English throne and during that time there were people who tried to help her escape. The English government worried in case Elizabeth was assassinated by Catholics who might try to put Catholic Mary on the English throne. Mary was kept under heavy guard.

JAMES VI
Plots Against the Child King

Scotland once more had a child on the throne and suffered from the power struggles of the barons and nobles. There were many plots to kidnap the young King James VI. His childhood was filled with fear. Two of his regents were shot, one died and the last was beheaded.

At one time there were two parliaments: one in Stirling supporting James the King, and one in Edinburgh supporting Mary the Queen. Queen Elizabeth sent troops to support James's men. In 1573 they used great cannons against Edinburgh Castle and after 11 days Mary's supporters were defeated.

Young James VI

A Lonely Childhood

Young James had a strict upbringing under Protestant lords. He learnt Latin, Greek, French as well as History and Politics. He studied Arithmetic, Composition, Geography and Astronomy. By the time he was 16, James was one of the best educated kings in Europe. His teacher was George Buchanan, a man who followed the teachings of John Knox.

Buchanan hated Mary and taught James that she was the enemy of Scotland. He taught James that kings were the servants of the people and that the people had the right to get rid of bad kings. This was a very frightening thought for James.

He led a lonely life and spent a great deal of time reading. He had over 600 books. Through these books James learned ideas which were different from those of Knox and Buchanan. He learned that kings in other countries were not thought of as servants. Kings were above the people and the church. They had a right to rule, given to them by God. It was a Divine Right.

James knew that once he was old enough to rule he would make laws to control the people and the church. He also wanted to protect himself from assassins and traitors.

James VI, King of Scotland

Mary Queen of Scots was executed on 8 February 1587, on the orders of Queen Elizabeth. James was 21 and two years late he married Anne of Denmark. For 14 years James VI ruled as King of Scotland.

Feuds and Fears

During this time he tried to control the feuding families in the Borders. The new Earl of Bothwell tried to attack James several times and Catholic earls plotted with Spain to remove James from the throne.

James was a fearful and superstitious man in spite of his education. During this time he wrote a book about demons. All over Scotland the torture and burning of "witches" began. For his young son, he wrote a book about kingship which said that kings were chosen by God and could only be judged by God. James truly believed this.

King James at a witch trial

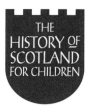

Law and Order

James ruled while Scotland was at peace. Throughout the land he began his work of reform and development. He was a strong king. Instead of fighting the earls and barons who opposed him James kept them out of the Government. Trouble makers were exiled abroad. Those who worked for the king became rich and powerful. Those who did not support the king were not as rich and had no power.

Exploring The New World

The 16th Century was an age of great discovery. Explorers from Spain and Portugal had sailed round the southern point of Africa and discovered the New World. Their sailors brought back great wealth and many exotic fruits and plants. Sir Francis Drake and Sir Walter Raleigh sailed from England and brought fame and wealth to the court of Queen Elizabeth. The first settlements or colonies were set up as trading posts. Soon the markets of Scotland had a share of goods such as sugar, chocolate and tobacco for sale.

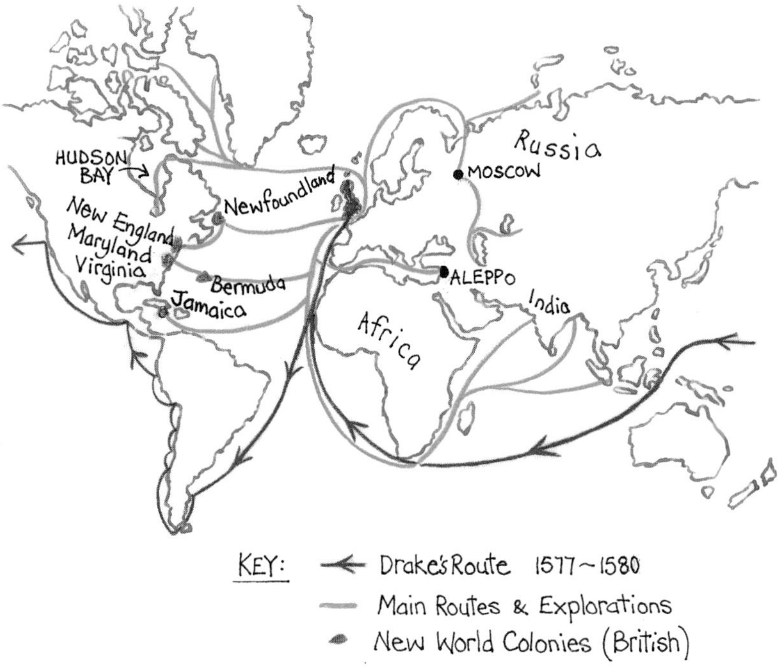

Trade and the Burghs

Peace between Scotland and England meant that trade improved and the burghs became wealthy. Houses were built of stone rather than wood. Windows now had glass. Burgesses decorated the insides of their houses with brightly painted ceilings, rich tapestries and carved furniture. Outside, the streets were just as filthy as before. Coal mining became an important industry. Salt-herring and salmon remained two of Scotland's greatest exports to Europe along with wool and hides. Imports included timber, iron, copper, wine, spices, silk, flax, paper, tobacco and weapons.

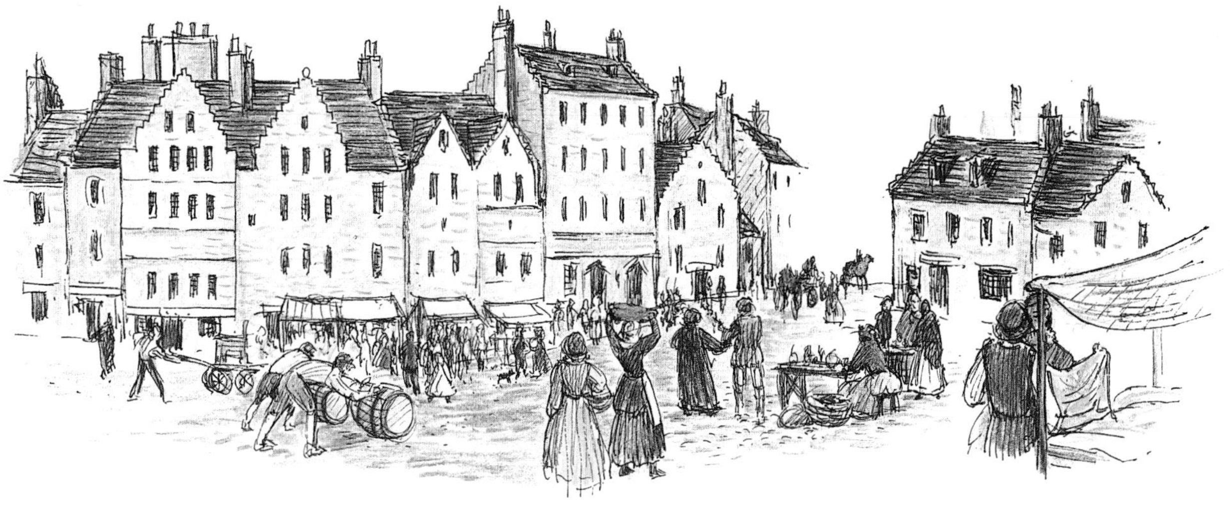

Life on the Land

Life for the Lowland peasants working the land remained the same. Since James did not want trouble between England and Scotland, he controlled the Borders and prevented raiding parties. Peace meant that farmers could bring in crops and sometimes there was extra to sell. The way the land was worked did not change however.

Life in the Highlands hardly changed at all. It was difficult for judges to travel into the remote glens. The clans continued their raiding and clan chiefs remained the "law" for their family groups.

The Kirk

The greatest change for the people was in the Church. Reformers such as John Knox and Andrew Melville had established a Presbyterian church. It was based on the teachings of

John Calvin from Switzerland. Instead of the ceremonies of the Catholic church there were sermons and psalm singing. Instead of the richly decorated cathedrals and abbeys there were plain, simple kirks. The Kirk was governed by a General Assembly, not by bishops living in fine houses. The king was not the head of the Kirk.

There were strict rules for the ministers, and the people of the Kirk also had to live under certain rules. There were rules forbidding bright clothes and jewels, and others which banned alehouses, gambling, dancing and music. On Sundays no work was allowed. The new church established schools and even the poor learnt to read and write. In 1582 Scotland's fourth university was established in Edinburgh.

James VI

THE STUARTS

In 1603 Elizabeth I of England died. She was the last of the Tudors. James Stewart became King of England – he was James I of England and James VI of Scotland. From this time on the Scottish spelling of Stewart was commonly replaced by the English version, Stuart, when used for the royal family.

JAMES, KING OF GREAT BRITAIN

James left for England on Sunday 3 April only a few days after hearing he was England's new king. He had a great vision of the uniting the kingdoms of Scotland,

England and Ireland. He called himself the King of Great Britain. In 1606 the Union flag came into being with the Saltire of St Andrew being added to the English flag. James liked his new found power and he wanted to use it to maintain peace and to make sure that he, the king, was free from any threat. Too many Scottish monarchs had lost their lives in violent struggles for power.

James and the Church

As King of England, James had great wealth and he was an important king in the eyes of other countries. He was head of the Church of England, which was called Episcopal because it was run by bishops. James controlled these bishops who wanted to stay in his favour. It was quite different from the way he was treated by the Scottish preachers. In the Church of Scotland the king was no more important than any other member of the church.

James and Andrew Melville argue in London

James decided that a United Kingdom needed a united church. The Church of Scotland should be more like the Church of England. He drew up the changes he wanted, including the introduction of bishops. James punished those preachers and members of the General Assembly who opposed him. Some, including Andrew Melville, leader of the Church of Scotland, were sent into exile for treason. By 1610 Scotland had bishops though they did not control the church in the same way as they did in England. By forcing his changes upon the Scottish church, James upset many of the Scots. They refused to obey.

James was very interested in religion and he also ordered a new version of the Bible to be translated from Latin into English. This Holy Bible became known as the King James Bible. It was used in churches throughout England and Scotland and later throughout the world.

The Years of Peace

James removed the custom duties. These were taxes paid on goods which crossed the borders between England and Scotland. He improved law and order more than any other Scottish king. There were courts twice a year in every county and Justices of the Peace could try cases for minor offences. While the distant Highlands remained unchanged, the Borders were quiet. Scotland knew real peace for well over 20 years.

James died on 27 March 1625. He had been James VI of Scotland for 58 years and James I of England for 22 years.

CHARLES I

James was succeeded by his 25 year old son, Charles I. Charles only lived in Scotland until he was four. Though he grew up very well educated, he knew little about his native homeland. To Charles, the role of king was a sacred duty and no-one should oppose their king. Charles, like his father, felt that the Church had a duty to support the king.

Charles I and the Church of Scotland

Charles knew that Scottish nobles had taken over the old Catholic church properties and lands during the Reformation. The properties were meant to support the church. Charles ordered the Act of Revocation which made the lands held by the nobles "crown land". The rent money had to go to the Scottish church. In this way Charles could pay the bishops and ministers. It took many years to settle. It made the nobles and landowners of Scotland suspicious of their new king.

Charles I

Charles Crowned in Scotland

Charles came to Edinburgh to be crowned King of Scotland eight years after being crowned in England. He wanted to impress the Scots and organised a grand coronation service. He had choirs and processions and the ministers wore fine garments but, his coronation service only reminded the Scots of the old Catholic ways.

The Book of Common Prayer

Like James, Charles planned to make the Scottish kirk more like the English church. He ordered a new Scottish prayer book to be written. He did not ask for advice or agreement from the General Assembly.

In 1637 the Book of Common Prayer and the King James Bible appeared. Charles had commanded the use of the Book of Common Prayer. This made the Scots angry. On Sunday 23 July 1637 in the High Church of St Giles there was a riot. As the Dean began to read from the book the people rose up to protest. A woman threw a stool at the Dean and when the Bishop of Edinburgh tried to calm the crowd there was an uproar. People spoke out about the hated bishops and fighting broke out.

Armed guards were called into St Giles to control the crowd. It was only the first of many public demonstrations which spread across the country. Peasants, burgesses and nobles were united; the Scottish people would not accept English rule over their church. Some people did not mind bishops while others did not mind the new prayer book, but they agreed on three points. They opposed the Catholic church of Rome, they supported the new Protestant faith and they were loyal to the king.

THE COVENANT

On 28 February 1638, in Greyfriars Kirkyard, a group of nobles signed an agreement called the National Covenant of Scotland. It listed all the Acts of Parliament proving the Scottish kirk was lawful. It was a statement about the rights and freedom of the Scots and their loyalty to the king. It was as important as the Declaration of Arbroath. It was carried across the country and thousands of people added their signatures, ministers, poor folk, nobles and burgesses. They became known as the Covenanters.

Signing the
Covenant

The Covenanters called a General Assembly in November 1638 in Glasgow. They abolished bishops, the new book of prayer and Charles's other plans for the church. They raised an army.

The Covenanters Fight for the Kirk

The Army of the Covenanters was led Alexander Leslie. His soldiers were experienced men who had been fighting in the Thirty Years War in Europe. They were supported by the people who paid for their weapons. They were fighting for freedom. Charles raised an army to put down the rebels but his men were no match for the Covenanters. His men were not trained and they were not well paid. In order to gain time, Charles promised to come to Scotland to meet with the Parliament and the Assembly. Both sides were to disband their armies. Charles did not keep his promises.

Earl of Montrose

Charles Forced to Accept the Covenant

A new Scottish army led by James Graham, Earl of Montrose, marched into England. By August 1640 the Covenanters had defeated the king's army and reached Newcastle. This time they wanted to speak to the English Parliament because they did not trust the king. A treaty was finally agreed by June 1641 and the king was forced to accept the terms of the General Assembly.

The Covenanters had won a great victory for the freedom of their church but, soon they were disagreeing amongst themselves. There was a struggle for power. Some wanted to get rid of the king even though the Covenant demanded loyalty to the king. People were being forced to sign the Covenant. Montrose was not happy. He had been the first to sign the Covenant and remained loyal to the king.

Royalist

Charles and the English Parliament

By this time Charles was in deep trouble with the English parliament. He had disbanded Parliament in 1629 and tried to rule without it for a time. He believed he ruled by Divine Right, that his power was given to him by God and that he could do no wrong. Now he wanted Parliament to raise money for his army. It would not. Instead Charles was told that Parliament, and not the king, should control the army, church and government of the country.

Civil War in England

Roundhead

Charles decided to fight his opponents. By August 1642 England was at war with itself, a Civil War. On one side there were the Parliamentarians and on the other side, the king's army, the Royalists.

Both sides wanted help from Scotland. The Scots demanded a Scottish-style church in England in return for their assistance. Since the Parliamentarians agreed and signed the Solemn League and Covenant, the Scots Covenanting Army joined that side. The English Parliamentarians also promised to pay the Scots for their soldiers.

In 1644 Alexander Leslie led the Covenanting Scots against the king's army, the Royalists. They joined Oliver Cromwell and the Parliament's troops who were called Roundheads because of their helmets. At Marston Moor near York, the Scots fought a brave battle and defeated Charles's northern army.

MONTROSE

James Graham, Earl of Montrose, chose to fight for King Charles and the Royalists. Montrose believed the king had granted all that the original Covenant had demanded in 1641. What was most important to him was loyalty. He and others had signed the Covenant agreeing to defend the king, to defend the new church as well as the laws of the land and the freedom of the people. Montrose felt that many of the Covenanters were now disloyal to the Covenant.

He met with Charles who made him Lieutenant General of the King's Forces in Scotland. Montrose returned to Scotland with just two friends He had to raise his own army. Civil War came to Scotland.

Montrose fought in the old Scots way

Montrose Wins Scotland

Montrose was a leader as powerful and brave as Wallace. He fought with a small band of men and faced great odds without equipment and with little support. He fought in the old Scots way, using the rugged Highland passes, the mists and bogs as a way to defeat and weary his enemy. His men were strong hardy Highlanders and the wild Irish men led by Coll Keitach. They crossed the country in blizzards in deepest winter to launch surprise attacks on the Covenanting forces. Within a year Montrose had control over the whole of Scotland.

Montrose Defeated

In September 1645 he turned south, planning to go into England to help the King's Forces there. Montrose got no further than Selkirk where a great Covenanting army, led by Leslie, stopped him. Montrose was outnumbered but his men fought bravely until few were left. They persuaded Montrose to leave the field to reach safety.

The Covenanting ministers took revenge in the name of God. They punished those who had supported Montrose: 300 men were hacked to pieces at Dunaverty Fort, 200 of James Lamont's men were captured, 36 were hanged from one tree while the others were butchered or buried alive.

Charles I Surrenders

In May 1646 Charles I surrendered to a Scottish Covenanting army which was in England and ordered all his armies to disband. He ordered Montrose to do the same and to leave the country for fear of his life. Montrose went to Holland which was a Protestant country. Here he met Charles's son. Young Prince Charles had been sent out of England during the wars.

Charles Refuses the Covenanting Terms

The Covenanters could not get Charles to accept the Solemn League and Covenant which had been signed by Parliament. They could not get the English parliament to pay the expenses which had been promised to Scotland. In the end the army had to return to Scotland. They handed Charles over to the English parliament but only after a promise that no harm would come to the king.

Charles I Executed by the English Parliament

In Scotland the Earl of Argyll took control of the country while in England, Oliver Cromwell became more powerful, leading the Parliament's forces, or Roundheads. On 30 January 1649, four days after a trial for treason, the English parliament beheaded the king, Charles I.

The Scots had lost their king, executed by the English, without their consent. It seemed there could not be peace between the two countries. Even Argyll and those who fought with the English against the king now prepared for war against England. They immediately proclaimed Charles II, King of Scotland, and called him back from Holland.

Charles I executed

CHARLES II

Charles II was very cautious about the Scots. He wasn't sure he could trust people who had handed his father over to the English Roundheads. He was not sure about accepting the Solemn League and Covenant either. Charles felt he could trust Montrose, however.

Montrose Betrayed and Executed

Montrose returned to Scotland for his new king. He raised a small army in Orkney and crossed to the mainland. At Carbisdale, on the Dornoch Firth on 27 April 1650, his army was surprised and defeated. Montrose was betrayed by Macleod of Assynt for £25,000 a few days later. He was taken to Edinburgh. His officers were axed or

Charles II

guillotined. The men of Orkney who had fought with him were sent as slaves into the coal mines of Fife.

James Graham, Earl of Montrose and Viceroy of Scotland, was hanged like a common criminal in Edinburgh on 21 May 1650. Before he died he spoke to the crowds. He said he had been loyal to the Covenant. He had fought those who took sides with England against Scotland's king. His body was cut up and sent to the gates of Stirling, Glasgow, Perth and Aberdeen. His head was put on a spike above the Tollbooth. The crowds in Edinburgh who were there to throw stones and cheer could only weep. Like Wallace, Montrose died loyal to his king and for freedom and justice.

Montrose hanged

Charles Crowned King of Scotland.

Charles II arrived in Scotland. He was crowned at Scone on 1 January 1651. Charles had signed the Covenant but only as a way to gain support.

Cromwell

Cromwell, Lord Protector of England, led his forces against the Covenanters in Scotland. After a number of battles Cromwell defeated the Scots and Charles left the country again. For 8 years Scotland was ruled by Cromwell who declared England and Scotland to be a single country, a Commonwealth. Cromwell died in 1658.

Oliver Cromwell

Scotland after Cromwell

During the years of Cromwell's "Protectorate" Scotland had lost trade and been taxed heavily. Cheaper goods from England put small Scottish industries out of business. Although Scotland was free to trade abroad she had lost many ships during the war. England had a great naval fleet which established English power all around the world.

THE COLONIES

After the great voyages of discovery, colonies or settlements in Africa, India and the New World (north and south America) were established. The islands of the Caribbean were known as the West Indies. Each of the major European countries had colonies of their own. Spain for example had some of its colonies in Southern America. France and England had colonies in Northern America.

The Colonies

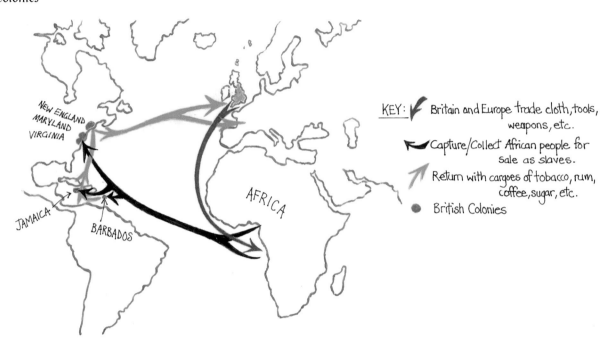

The Settlers

The people who settled the colonies were sometimes adventurers looking for gold and silver. More often, settlers were looking for a better way of life and land of their own. Many had escaped religious persecution. New England was settled by Puritans in 1625. Maryland (1632) and Carolina (1663) were colonies settled by Catholics.

Later, the slave trade brought black Africans to work the plantations of America and the West Indies. Transportation became a form of punishment in Britain. Criminals were "transported" to the colonies to work as slaves or convicts. Other prisoners, such as the Covenanters, were also transported.

New Trade

In the colonies, new foods such as potatoes, coffee, tea, chocolate, and sugar had been discovered. Cotton, tobacco, skins and rum were traded. The colonists sold their goods to trading companies which had fleets of ships. The East India Company (1559) controlled trade in the Far East. The Virginia Company (1606) traded with the colonies of northern America.

A Scottish Colony Fails

In 1629 the Scots attempted a settlement in Nova Scotia, then held by the French. The leader, David Kirke, gained control of Port Royal and Quebec but in 1632 Charles I returned the territory to the French. The Scots had no trading companies and no colonies and could not have a share of the new wealth.

Nova Scotia

THE RESTORATION

In 1660 Charles II was "restored" as King of England, Scotland and Ireland. The years of his rule became known as the Restoration Period.

Trade

Almost immediately the English Navigation Acts of 1660 and 1663 affected the Scots. By law, English colonies were only allowed to trade with English merchants. The Scots were foreigners and not allowed to trade with English colonies. In spite of the Acts, some trade was established since America wanted Scottish goods.

Charles II and the Kirk

Charles II ruled with a strong grip over both Parliament and the church. From London he ruled Scotland in the same way. Charles was not interested in the Covenant and in 1661 he called the Scottish parliament. He abolished all the Acts which had been passed since 1633.

Charles was now head of the Church of Scotland and England. He brought back the bishops to replace the General Assembly under the control of Parliament.

Conventicles

Some of the strict Covenant ministers left their kirks and took their followers, or congregations, into the fields to pray rather than accept the king's changes. These meetings were called Conventicles and were made illegal. Soldiers were sent in to break up the meetings.

Uprisings

Charles ruled Scotland using powerful men such as John Middleton, the Earl of Rothes and the Duke of Lauderdale as his high commissioners. Rothes was harsh in his dealing with the Covenanters and there were revolts. In 1666 a band of about 3,000 marched from Ayrshire to Edinburgh. At Rullion Green the march ended in bloodshed and hangings. Many who escaped death were sent off to the West Indies as slaves for the plantations.

One uprising involved a group of people who called themselves the "Society Folk". Their preacher was Richard Cameron and they became known as Cameronians. They believed they were the true Presbyterian Church of Scotland. They disowned the king at a meeting in Sanquhar in June 1680. They were made outlaws. Over the next few years the Cameronians battled with the king's troops.

JAMES II OF ENGLAND AND VII OF SCOTLAND

Charles II died on 6 February 1685 and was succeeded by his brother James. James II of England and VII of Scotland was a Catholic. He refused to take the oath to defend the Protestant religion.

James II

James and Religion

James soon passed a law which made it treason to support the Covenant and to attend Conventicles. He hunted down the Cameronians. However, two years later in 1687, he passed a law granting "freedom of worship" to all people. He wanted Catholics to be able to worship once more. His law also allowed the Presbyterians to leave the Episcopal Church of Scotland run by Charles's bishops and they returned to their kirks with their preachers.

James put his Catholic friends into high positions and set up a Catholic church at Holyrood. People worried about how long they would be "free" to worship in their own churches. They knew the Protestants in France were being hunted down. They feared the Pope in Rome would again control their lives.

William and Mary

In June 1688 the king's son was born. In England there was great fear because this child meant that England's next king would also be Catholic. Leaders in England decided to make sure that did not happen.

WILLIAM AND MARY

The English contacted the Protestant Prince William of Orange in Holland who was married to James's Protestant daughter, Mary. They asked William and Mary to rule over Protestant England.

William offered to replace King James and rule Scotland as well. The Scots were not prepared to make up their minds so quickly. James was the crowned king and, so far at least, people were free to worship as they pleased.

William and Mary Crowned in England

William arrived in England with a large army in November 1688. Much of the army was made up of Scots Covenanters who had been exiled. There was no battle. King James was allowed to escape to France. In February 1689, William and Mary were crowned King and Queen of England.

Scotland's Terms for the Crown

The Scots did not offer their crown immediately but they did ask William to take over the Government until they could choose a ruler. There was confusion among the people. When James fled to France many felt he had abdicated, given up his right to rule.

William called a Convention of Estates in Edinburgh to decide who should wear the crown. The Convention was made up of leading nobles, churchmen and business men. They had a letter from William and one from James. Each wanted to be the king.

William promised in his letter to defend the Protestant faith. James sent a letter commanding loyalty and support from his subjects even if that meant they would have to become Catholic. James even threatened those who did not support him. It was not difficult for the Convention to choose William.

The Convention of Estates

William and Mary were offered the Crown of Scotland because James had failed his duties as king. He had failed to take the oath which was required under Scottish law. He had no respect for the laws and liberties of the land. Before William was crowned King of Scotland in May 1689, he had to agree to all the rules set down by the Convention. The rules were different from those for England. They protected the Church of Scotland which was to be governed by the General Assembly, not the king. There would be no more bishops.

THE JACOBITES

At this point begins a new period in Scottish history overshadowed by the Jacobites. The Jacobites were those who supported the Stuart king, James VII. They were not all Catholics but they believed James to be the Scottish king. They were called Jacobites because Jacobus is Latin for James. Those who supported William were known as Williamites.

Bonnie Dundee

One of the first Jacobites was John Graham of Claverhouse, Viscount Dundee, sometimes known as "Bonnie Dundee". He went into the Highlands to raise an army to fight for James. He gathered about 2,000 men from the Donald, Cameron, Stewarts and MacLean clans. Dundee led them south to Perthshire.

Killiecrankie

On 27 July 1689 Dundee's Highlanders waited at Killiecrankie, a steep pass in the mountains. King William's troops of about 4,000 men were led by General Hugh Mackay. As they came out of the pass they were slaughtered in just a few minutes in a charge by the wild Highland men. Mackay escaped with some survivors but Dundee was shot and killed.

Bonnie Dundee

Without a leader the Highlanders moved south, not to fight for the cause of James, but to plunder and raid. They got to Dunkeld where a new Covenanting army made up of the Cameronians defended the town. The Highlanders gave up and returned home leaving no one to fight for James.

Killiecrankie

William Controls the Highlanders

William decided he must gain control over the Highlands to prevent more rebellions. He offered a pardon to those who had fought against him. In August 1691 the Government instructed all the clans to swear loyalty to King William before New Year's Day 1692 or face punishment.

The clan chiefs sent messages to King James in France asking him to release them from the oath they had sworn to him. James released the clans from their Oath of Loyalty but his message did not reach Scotland until late in December. There was little time for the chiefs to reach the sheriffs to swear their new oaths to William.

One clan chief, Alasdair MacDonald of Glencoe, made his journey on New Years' Eve. He reached Fort William only to find the sheriff was not there. He went on to Inveraray, 80 miles away, in the winter snow and gales arriving on 3 January. But the deputy sheriff would not take his oath until 6 January.

MacDonald
of Glencoe

Massacre at Glencoe

The Government decided to make an example of this clan. At the end of January 1692, a regiment of Argyll's men, led by Captain Robert Campbell moved into Glencoe. They sheltered with the MacDonalds in their homes and shared their food. Then, on 13 February, as day broke, the soldiers massacred the sleeping clansfolk in their beds including some women and children. Many of those who escaped died in the harsh winter conditions in the mountains.

Scotland was angry and many people lost faith in this new king and his government.

Massacre at
Glencoe

LIFE IN 17TH CENTURY SCOTLAND

Scotland at the end of the 17th Century was a poor country. Most of the population were still peasant farmers living in one-roomed cottages. They lived on what they could grow on their rigs. There had been no improvements to farming methods. At any time landlords could evict peasants from their homes and land.

Great sheep farms took up much of the border lands and rich farm lands had been developed around Inverness, Moray, Aberdeen and Dundee. Farmers in these places sometimes had crops which they could sell.

Education

In 1696 the Scottish Parliament passed an Act which provided schools in every parish or district. The landowners and tenants had to pay the schoolmaster. Classes were often held in barns or byres where the children sat on the floor. Teachers were poorly paid and sometimes had to live with one of the farmers or even take up extra work. Children learned how to read and write, at least in the Lowlands and in the burghs.

The Highlands

The harsh life of the Highlanders changed very little. The land was not suitable for farming and little was grown. Raising cattle for beef was the main livelihood. Though many of the Highland chiefs were educated, cattle raiding and feuding continued. Many of the clans were still loyal to King James. The Highlands remained isolated.

The Burghs

The burghs had become bigger. Edinburgh and Glasgow were the main centres for spinning and weaving. Glasgow had been rebuilt with stone houses and wide streets after a great fire in 1677. Soap and sugar became important industries there. Aberdeen also had a wool industry while Perth and Dundee were centres for the Scottish linen trade. They were the next largest burghs. The fishing ports were Greenock, Anstruther, Crail and Dunbar as well as Musselburgh and Leith. Coal was mined around the Forth and also round Irvine and Glasgow.

Trade

Trade had suffered during the wars. The English Navigation Acts of 1660 and 1663 had limited Scottish trade with English colonies in the New World. England grew wealthy because of her imported goods and she developed manufacturing industries. Cheap goods such as linen, pottery, pins, needles, pots and pans became available. The Scots had to import these from England.

Starvation

Three years after the massacre at Glencoe, Scotland faced starvation when crops failed in bad weather. Between 1695 and 1702 thousands died of disease and hunger. Many died trying to reach towns like Edinburgh and Stirling. Lime pits were dug to bury the dead. The winter weather brought blizzards and freezing conditions and even the landlords had no money or food to help the poor.

Improving Trade

During 1695 the Scottish Parliament passed many Acts to try to improve the economy. The Bank of Scotland was set up. Another Act set up a national trading company which was called the Company of Scotland.

Merchants discussing trade

The Scots knew they had to set up colonies of their own to increase trade. At first King William agreed to this and money for the company was raised in both England and Scotland. The company planned to trade with Africa, America and Asia.

But William was not to be trusted. When powerful businessmen in England thought they would lose trade to Scotland, William and the Parliament blocked the Scots. When Scotland tried to raise support in other countries, William blocked them again.

The Darien Scheme

Eventually the Scots raised the money by themselves. The plan was to send settlers to build a trading port at Darien on the Panama, between North and South America. From there, trade could be opened up throughout the Caribbean and even beyond, with countries such as China. The venture became known as the Darien Scheme. It seemed to be the only way to help Scotland to recover from terrible poverty.

On 14 July 1698 four ships with 1,500 settlers sailed for their new home in Darien. They took their supplies and goods for trading. They had no idea what life would be like in the tropics.

New Caledonia

KEY: ● New Edinburgh
◉ Darien ~renamed New Caledonia

No Support from William

Then Spain declared that Darien was their territory. William did not want Spain to know he had approved of the Company of Scotland. Because he did not want war with Spain, he ordered English settlements already in North America and the Caribbean not to give any help to the Scottish settlers.

The settlers were not prepared for conditions in Darien. Within less than a year half of them had died of tropical diseases. The survivors set sail for home though only one ship reached Scotland. Before it arrived, however, four more ships had already left Scotland.

This second expedition tried to rebuild the settlement but they were attacked by the Spaniards. They fought off two attacks but the third attack was a siege and after a month, the hungry, sick Scots surrendered in March 1700. The Spaniards sent the survivors back on their ships. Very few reached Scotland after the long sea journey.

The Darien disaster

The Darien Scheme was a great disaster for Scotland. Only 300 of the 2,500 men women and children survived. Nine ships had been lost and most of the money was gone. The Scots blamed William and his government. There were riots in Edinburgh. The Scottish parliament did not want to pay William's taxes. Throughout Scotland there was a feeling of distrust for the English government and for William. When William died suddenly in March 1702, few Scots mourned him.

THE UNION
Choosing the Future Monarch

Anne Stuart

Anne Stuart, daughter of James VII was made queen. All of her children had died. The English parliament had to decide who would be king or queen after Anne. They did not ask the Scots. The German Princess Sophia of Hanover, granddaughter of James I (VI of Scotland) was chosen. The Scots wanted to choose their own monarch.

The English parliament feared Scotland might become a separate kingdom again. The Scots might choose the exiled James as king. The real fear

72

was that Scotland would then join France in the war against England. They banned all Scottish cattle, linen and coal until the Scots agreed to accept the English choice of monarch.

Scotland was too poor to face a war. The years of famine and the Darien disaster had left the country without money and without trade. They needed to trade with England.

The Terms of the Union

In April 1706 representatives from Scotland and England began to draw up agreements to unite the two countries. In October 1706 the terms were presented to the Scottish parliament.

Sophia of Hanover

Scotland was to have equal trading rights and a payment of £400,000 from England to help make up for the Darien disaster. The Scots would keep their Scottish Law and Law Courts. England would have the choice of Sophia of Hanover and her Protestant heirs on the British throne. The united parliament would have 190 English Lords and 16 Scottish Lords. In the House of Commons there would be 513 English and Welshmen and 45 Scots. There was to be a common currency, weights and measures.

Great Britain, a New Nation

The Scottish people were angry because the terms of the Union seemed to be bad for Scotland. There were riots and fierce arguments in the Scottish parliament. Some Scots were bribed to support the Union. By 19 March 1707 the terms were agreed. On 25 March the last meeting of the Scottish parliament took place. On 1 May 1707 the two countries were united as Great Britain, a new nation.

The Scottish Parliament

Scotland's Trade Suffers

The Scots hoped they would now share in the wealth of the united nation. It was not to be. Scottish goods could not compete with the cheaper English goods and many folk went out of business. The Scottish linen trade was heavily taxed but the English woollen trade was not. Scottish coal exported to Ireland was taxed but not English coal. The salt tax almost ruined the herring fishers.

Fish wives

During this time the Scots were called to fight in the war against France. They had little say in whether they wanted war or peace. The Scots grew more angry.

UNREST AND THE JACOBITES

In 1708 the French helped in a plan to bring Catholic James VIII, the uncrowned son of James VII, back to Scotland. He was to claim the crown of the United Kingdom. James VIII arrived with a fleet of ships but, he was easily turned back by a British fleet. There was little support from the mainland. Most of the Scots certainly did not want a Catholic king.

In 1714 Queen Anne died and the German son of Sophia of Hanover became the new king, George I. A year later, in 1715 there was a Jacobite rebellion led by the Earl of Mar, John Erskine, who had failed to win favour with the new king.

James VIII

The '15 Uprising

Mar raised about 6,000 clansmen. The Jacobites seized Inverness and Perth. Stirling Castle was held for the Government by the Duke of Argyll who blocked the Jacobites from moving into the Lowlands.

A second Jacobite army of 2,000 outwitted the government troops and crossed the Firth of Forth in small boats at night. They joined the Border Jacobites and marched into England down to Preston. However, almost 500 of the Highlanders grew tired of being so far away and returned to their glens. After a two day battle in November the Jacobite army was defeated in Preston.

On that same day, 13 November 1715, the Earl of Mar brought his Jacobites to Sheriffmuir

KEY:
⌇ The Border
← Main Jacobite Army
→ Borlum's Route
✗ Battle of Sherrifmuir

near Stirling. He would have to defeat the Duke of Argyll and the Union army to gain control over the Lowlands. There was a furious battle in which both sides lost many men. The Jacobites were defeated. When James VIII arrived in Scotland in December, the cause was already lost. He and the Earl of Mar escaped back to France in February 1716.

A One Day Rebellion

In 1719 the Spanish saw a chance to gain some control over the united kingdoms of Scotland and England. They sent a fleet with a promise of 5,000 troops and weapons for 30,000. But bad weather meant only 300 troops landed to meet a small gathering of Highlanders. The rebellion was at an end after one day's fighting when the Highlanders left the Spaniards to surrender to government troops.

Controlling the Highlands

It was clear to the Government that the Highlanders had to be controlled. It was the same problem that every ruler of Scotland had faced through the centuries. The Highlanders lived in a wild and rugged land where they could hide in the glens and misty mountains. It was a land of small hamlets and few roads. The Highlanders could gather and come swarming out against their enemies but no army could march into the Highlands against them.

Wade's Roads

The Government sent General Wade to build roads and bridges. Over the next few years, roads reached deeper and deeper into the Highland Glens. The roads stretched between the government strongholds at Fort William, Fort George and Fort Augustus. Now the armies could move quickly between the fortresses and patrol further into the glens.

KEY: △ Government Forts and Barracks ⟶

Wade's Roads

1 FORT GEORGE	5 RUTHVEN
2 INVERNESS	6 BERNERA
3 FORT AUGUSTUS	7 INVERSNAID
4 FORT WILLIAM	8 INVERARAY

The Highland Regiments

The Government also recruited clansmen into the army to help keep the peace. They wore a kilt of government green and became known as the Black Watch. They were usually men from those clans loyal to King George and the Government. The Jacobites, those clansmen loyal to the Stuarts, hid their weapons and waited for a chance to free Scotland from the English and the Union.

Black Watch

BONNIE PRINCE CHARLIE

Bonnie
Prince Charlie

Charles Edward Stewart, (or Stuart) often called Bonnie Prince Charlie, was counting upon these Jacobites when he sailed from France to Scotland in 1745. He wanted to raise an army and take back the throne for his father, James.

When the prince arrived on the Isle of Eriskay on 23 July with his few companions, the Clan Chief told them to go back to France. Charles bravely said he would not return and he sailed to the mainland.

The '45

On 19 August Charles raised his flag. The first of the Highlanders, the Camerons, marched out of the glens to join the prince. More joined the army as the days went by. King George II and the government put a price of £30,000 on the prince's head. Sir John Cope was sent with the government army to end the rebellion.

Prince Charles now had an army of 2,000. He used Wade's roads to move quickly across Scotland. He took Perth on 4 September and headed south towards Edinburgh. Sir John Cope had been left behind in Inverness. He marched to Aberdeen from where he and his men set sail for Edinburgh.

The gathering of the clans

Prince Charles takes Edinburgh

There was panic and fear in the hearts of many folk as Bonnie Prince Charlie and the Highlanders arrived at Edinburgh, still a walled city. The volunteer guards did not want to fight and Cope's men were unable to land due to bad weather.

On 17 September 1745, Edinburgh surrendered and Charles proclaimed his father, King James VIII of Scotland and III of England.

On the same day, Cope finally managed to land his men at Dunbar and he began the march towards Edinburgh. Three days later, on 20 September, Charles and the Highland army took him by surprise at Prestonpans. The government army fled as the wild Highlanders attacked. Charles now held Scotland and there was real fear in England.

Charles did not move south for several weeks. He was unable to gather much support in the Lowlands. By the time he marched across the border the government had been able to gather a strong army.

Charles enters the Netherbow Port

The Jacobites in England

Wade, now Marshal Wade, commanded a government force at Newcastle. The Duke of Cumberland held a government force in the south of England. Cumberland was the third son of George II and a cousin to Bonnie Prince Charlie.

Charles and the Scottish Jacobites marched deep into England taking Penrith, Lancaster, Preston and Manchester. Along the way he found only 200 English Jacobites to join his men. He wanted to march on London but a large army had gathered there. The armies of Cumberland and Wade were also waiting to move against him. Charles had to return to the safety of Scotland. It was early in December. The Highlanders easily overran Cumberland's troops near Preston on 17 December and returned to Scotland.

Main sites of the '45

Key: ⚔ BATTLES
      ✱ SIEGE
      ···· Border

The Return to Scotland

On 17 January 1746 the Jacobites met Cumberland's men at Falkirk. The Highlanders stood their ground in the face of a cavalry charge but at the very last minute the English charge was brought down by musket fire on each side of the field. It had been a trap. The Highlanders charged and within minutes they had won the day. Cumberland's defeated army ran.

In spite of this victory the Jacobite cause seemed doomed to failure. There was no new support. The weary Highlanders were returning to their glens again. Lowland Scots were joining the government forces.

Duke of Cumberland

Culloden

On 16 April 1746 the prince's tired and hungry army waited in the wind and rain on Culloden Moor near Inverness. About 5,000 Highlanders faced the Duke of Cumberland himself with an army of 9,000. Cumberland also had modern artillery and about 800 mounted Dragoons. Scots loyal to King George formed part of this army. Cumberland was determined to end Highland rebellions forever.

Charles was advised against fighting at Culloden. The moor was flat and the weather was bad and his men were tired and hungry. He did not listen. He stayed to fight. The Jacobite lines were broken by heavy cannon fire. Their charge was brave but not strong enough against a stronger army of fresh soldiers with bayonets.

The Jacobites eventually turned to escape but they were cut down. Even the wounded and dying were bayoneted by Cumberland's men. Between 1,000 and 2,000 Jacobites died. Cumberland wanted the rebellion totally crushed and he would not take prisoners. The killing went on long after the battle and Cumberland became known as the "Butcher".

Battle of Culloden

Prince Charles Hidden and Rescued

After Culloden, Cumberland's men terrorised the Highland folk. They burnt homes and slaughtered those who either could not or would not reveal the whereabouts of Bonnie Prince Charlie.

The prince was hidden by loyal clans and moved from place to place away from the bands of murdering soldiers. They risked their lives and their lands

Charles escapes

if they were caught. One of the many who helped the prince was Flora MacDonald of South Uist. When she feared the soldiers were too close she disguised the prince as her serving maid. She took him to Skye in her boat. Later she was arrested and sent to prison. By then Charles had escaped. On 19 September he was rescued and taken back to France.

Flora MacDonald

After Culloden

In the months after Culloden over 100 Highlanders were executed. Many more were killed by soldiers who burned down homes and stole anything of value. More than 1,000 people were sent to the plantations in the Caribbean and many of these died on the voyage. Thousands of the Highlanders' cattle were stolen and driven south along with hundreds of the tough Highland ponies, flocks of sheep and goats. The Highlanders faced starvation.

Laws to Keep the Peace

In Parliament, laws were made to prevent the Highland Clans from gathering strength again. The chief was no longer the law of his clan. Jacobite clan chiefs lost their lands. All weapons had to be surrendered, on pain of death. Since the bagpipes were regarded as a weapon, they also had to be given up. Anyone wearing the tartan could be transported. All Scots were punished because of the Jacobite Rebellion. Yet many clans had not rebelled against the Government. There were more clans against the Jacobite cause than for it.

42nd Highlanders
in North
America, 1762

To make good use of the Highlanders, the Government recruited many men into the army to fight overseas. Here at least they could wear the tartan and win honour for themselves and their clans.

The hunt for Jacobites went on for over five years after Culloden. It was the last battle ever fought in the United Kingdom of Great Britain.

THE 18TH CENTURY

Four Kings Called George

With peace came change and improvement. The history of Scotland from this time on had more to do with the people than with kings and generals.

Between 1715 and 1830 the next four kings of Britain were all called George. This period of British history is called Georgian.

George I

George III

Times of Change

The 18th Century was a time of new thought and improvement throughout the world. This period of history is called the Enlightenment. It was also a time of revolutions. There were revolutions in agriculture and industry affecting the way people lived and revolutions in America and France which were about freedom.

George II

George IV

Times of War

During the 18th Century, Britain was at war for much of the time. In India, America and Canada there were battles with the French and Spanish over the colonies. In Europe, Britain was involved in a number of wars including the Seven Years War and in America there was the War of Independence. The French Revolution was followed by the Napoleonic Wars.

Britain had both the Navy and the Army to support and supply which was good for farming and industry. Farmers had no trouble selling their produce, cattle and sheep. Manufactured goods such as clothes and tools were required. Men were also needed and many of them came from the Highlands.

THE AGRICULTURAL REVOLUTION

Since the majority of people still lived on the land it was the Agricultural Revolution which had the first and most important affect on the lives of the people.

There were new ideas and improvements in farming for the first time in hundreds of years. Changes in England were making landowners wealthy. Scottish landowners saw these improvements when they travelled and used the new ideas on their own lands. In 1723 a "Society of Improvers" was set up to share ideas and to help Scotland improve farming methods.

Improving the Land

The changes took many years. Landowners who wanted to improve had to spend a great deal of money first. The landowner did away with the old ferm-touns and the runrig system of growing crops. He divided his land into larger farms with fields and built farm houses. He then rented the farm to a tenant farmer for a number of years. Because the land was improved he could charge a higher rent.

An improved farm

Improving the land involved many changes. Marshy land was drained so it could be planted with crops. Trees were planted, providing wind breaks to protect fields. Fields were fenced, or enclosed, and were fertilised.

A system called "crop rotation" was introduced to improve the soil. These crops were turnips, clover, barley and wheat, some of which animals could eat in winter. This meant cattle and sheep did not have to be killed and salted for winter. Potatoes were introduced and gradually became an important food for the people.

Life for the Farmers

Farmers living on improved farms had better crops and usually made a reasonable living for themselves. They had more comfortable homes to live in and good food to eat. Because they could rent the land for several years, the farmers felt it was worth working hard and making improvements.

There were still farmworkers who did not rent land. They had small cottages to live in and the tenant farmer paid them a wage. However, other improvements and new inventions which helped the farmer meant there was not so much work for farm labourers. These people had to look for work in the towns.

James Small's new plough and Jethro Tull's seed drill

The new metal plough could be used by one man with two horses. The seed drill planted seed in straight rows, saving seed and making weeding easier. A theshing mill saved flailing by hand. Farmers learned how to breed bigger cattle and sheep.

The general improvement in living standards meant the population was growing too. People lived longer and their babies and children had a better chance of survival.

Change in the Highlands

Life in the Highlands had always been hard but during the 18th Century the old pattern of life changed forever. Even before the Union many of the lairds and landowners moved to the cities and to London. After the Jacobite Rebellions of 1715 and 1745 there were Disarming Acts, laws to forbid men owning weapons. Many clan chiefs had been killed and others had lost their lands. The people on those lands had lost the heads of their families.

The First Emigrations

New landlords took over the glens. The old system of loyalty to a clan chief was broken down. The tacksmen were no longer needed to raise men for war. They could not make a living out of their tenant farmers who were now very poor. It was the tacksmen who organised the first emigrations of Highlanders to the colonies.

By 1773, 20,000 Highlanders had emigrated, searching for land of their own and a better way of life. Soldiers returning to Scotland from wars in the colonies encouraged their families and clansmen to emigrate to Canada. Many soldiers

had been given land in the colonies instead of pay. Their families were happy to leave the harsh life in Scotland. Others were driven to leave Scotland after years of famine and increasing rents.

Improvers in the Highlands

There were some landowners and clan chiefs who worried about the numbers of Highlanders leaving Scotland. The kelp industry earned a great amount money for

landlords. They tried to keep their tenants. The seaweed, or kelp, was collected and burned. The ashes were sent to soap and glass manufacturers until the industry collapsed in 1815 at the end of the Napoleonic Wars.

Gathering kelp

The Duke of Argyll tried to provide a base for herring fishing by building the town of Inveraray. Across Scotland many new villages were constructed and some chiefs tried to provide work for their tenants. Grantown-on-Spey was planned as an industrial town for the production of linen and woollen goods as well as the timber trade. Fishing stations were set up in Skye, at Ullapool, Tobermory and near Wick. Still the people left.

Main Highland towns

In Caithness Sir John Sinclair built the port of Scrabster and the new town of Thurso. He believed as many of the people as possible should stay on the land. He thought they should all keep some profitable sheep, as well as keeping cattle and growing some crops on newly improved large farms. Those who had to leave the land could find work in newly developed industries such as tanning, brewing and mining. Sinclair lost money trying to improve life for his tenants. His greatest problem was isolation. Caithness was hundreds of miles from the cities of Edinburgh, Glasgow and London. It cost too much to transport goods to these places.

In Sutherland the Marquis of Stafford, husband of the young Countess of Sutherland, began improvements. New towns with stone houses were built at Brora, Golspie and Helmsdale. Industries such as fishing, saltworks, mining and brewing were expanded. The people being cleared from the newly planned sheep runs were moved to these towns. Small areas of land along the coast were available for crofts, or small holdings. He built roads, bridges and inns.

Some clansfolk moved to the coast to make a new life. Some did not like fishing for a living and they missed the old ways of the land even though that life had been harsh. They booked places on the emigration ships.

Golspie, Sutherland

The Clearances

Many of the folk remained on the land until they were forced off. They did not own the land and they could not pay the rents. They had no rights to the land though they and their ancestors had worked for the clan chiefs and fought for them for generations. Leaving the land meant leaving the "family" and the Highlanders felt betrayed.

Landowners could make more money from sheep than from renting land to the clansmen. The new sheep were strong and could be bred for both meat and wool. They were the Cheviots and the Blackface Lintons. The Highlanders were evicted, cleared from their homes to make the land available for sheep. This period of "Improvement" became known as the Highland Clearances.

Evictions

Eventually, landowners enforced the evictions of those who refused to leave the land of their ancestors. Where there was likely to be trouble, soldiers were called in. Houses and crops were burnt so there would be nothing for the folk to come back to. Some of these evictions were carried out with great cruelty. The old and ill were turned out into bad weather. Those who resisted were beaten and forced to leave. The worst of these brutal evictions happened in Sutherland.

There was no where for the majority of people to go during later years of the Clearances. Some went to the towns and cities hoping to find work. Others sailed for the colonies. The Clearances went on from 1760 for over 100 years.

The Burnings

THE ENLIGHTENMENT
Education

The Enlightenment was sometimes called the Age of Reason, an age of new thinking. Scotland was one of the first countries in the world to believe in education for young children. The first schools set up by the new Church of Scotland in the 16th Century were mostly in the Lowlands. In 1696 there was an Education Act to make sure that all young children learnt to read and write. A special society was set up to run schools in the Highlands so that Gaelic speaking children also learnt English.

David Hume

Adam Smith

Scotland's Men of Science

During the 18th Century Scotland produced some of the world's greatest thinkers, writers and scientists. Most of them had only been to small parish schools. David Hume wrote books about the way people think and feel. This was the start of the science called Psychology. Adam Smith wrote about the importance of sharing wealth with the people who laboured to make the country rich. He was the founder of the science called Political Economy.

At Glasgow University, James Watt assisted Joseph Black who studied heat and discovered carbon dioxide. James Watt experimented with heat and the production of steam. Later James used the power of steam to drive machines.

James Watt

William Dick

There were great doctors as well. John and William Hunter studied at Glasgow and Edinburgh Universities and worked in London as surgeons and teachers. John's famous pupil was Edward Jenner who discovered the vaccine against small pox. William Dick studied the breeding of animals. In 1823 he founded the Edinburgh Veterinary College.

Scotland's Men of Letters

Robert Burns

Edinburgh became an important centre for publishing. There was a huge interest in the works of the old Scottish poets. Old songs were collected before they were "lost". Allan Ramsay, who was a bookseller, published some of these works. In 1728 Ramsay set up the first lending library in Scotland. Poets such as Robert Fergusson and Robert Burns came to Edinburgh and they were treated as celebrities. Walter Scott wrote poetry and novels and his works helped to make Scotland a "romantic" place to readers all over the world.

Allan Ramsay,
Senior

Allan Ramsay,
Artist

Walter Scott

THE
HISTORY OF
SCOTLAND
FOR CHILDREN

Scotland's Artists

There were many famous artists: Allan Ramsay son of the bookseller, John Burnet, Sir David Wilkie, Alexander Nasmyth and Sir Henry Raeburn. Some recorded the Scottish way of life and others painted dramatic scenery, called landscapes. Their work brought pictures of Scotland to a wider world.

Scotland's Architects

Great architects from Scotland worked all over Britain. The most famous were William Adam and his sons and the best known of these was Robert. He worked in the classical style of ancient Greece and Rome. He include the design of the interior decoration and furnishings in his plans for buildings.

Scotland's New Towns and Old Tenements

Robert Adam

By the middle of the 18th Century Edinburgh was overcrowded. The City Council held a competition for the best plan for a new town. It was won by James Craig who designed wide streets with parks and fine public buildings. The New Town was built in golden sandstone and the elegant houses had large windows and plenty of space. Robert Adam designed Charlotte Square and other buildings. It was very different from the old town with its tightly packed, tall buildings and dark wynds. The wealthy folk were happy to leave the crowded dirty tenements of the old town.

Walter Scott's house in Castle Street

Glasgow's wealthy people also built large and spacious homes for themselves away from the busy centre of the city. During the 18th Century Glasgow became the centre for trade in Scotland. Merchants exported linen, leather good, tools, pottery, glassware and furniture to the colonies. They imported sugar, tobacco, timber and fruits. So much money was made from tobacco that the merchants

Carlton Place, Glasgow

were called Tobacco Lords.

In both Edinburgh and Glasgow the old tenement buildings in the centres of the towns were filled with new tenants. They were mostly folk evicted from the land. They had come to the cities to find work. Whole families crowded into single rooms. With no running water and no toilets, living conditions in the old towns were unhealthy. The poor had little food and overcrowding led to diseases such as smallpox, cholera and typhus which killed thousands of people. The centres of the towns became slums.

Across the country smaller towns grew up wherever there was a chance for trade or the development of industry.

THE INDUSTRIAL REVOLUTION
The Linen Trade

During the 18th Century Scottish industries were mostly cottage industries and people worked in their own homes. Linen was an important industry for Scotland. The flax was delivered to the cottages by agents. The spinners made the yarn on spinning wheels and the weavers wove the cloth on looms. The agent then collected and paid for the finished cloth.

Cottage industry

Different parts of Scotland specialised in the type of cloth they made. In Fife they made coarse linen and canvas sails for the Navy. Dunfermline, in Fife, produced fine damask linens for table cloths. Perth produced sheets, muslin and calico. Dundee, Paisley and Glasgow were all important centres for the production of linen. Most of the linen was exported to the colonies in America.

The Cotton Industry

After the American War of Independence the linen trade collapsed. Cotton was being grown in America and it was cheaper than flax and easier to use. Soon, new inventions, the Flying Shuttle and the Spinning Jenny, speeded up the production of cotton cloth.

Factory industry

Richard Arkwright's invention in 1769, the Waterframe, changed the cotton industry from a cottage industry to factory industry. The machines were very expensive and they were too big for cottages.

The machines had to be put into mills built next to rivers, because the wheels were operated by running water. By 1781 James Watt had produced a steam engine to drive the wheels.

During the next 50 years about 200 mills were built in Scotland. Most owners of the mills took advantage of the poor to operate the machines. Women and children were used because they could be paid less. Mill workers lived in miserable conditions and worked long days.

Robert Owen

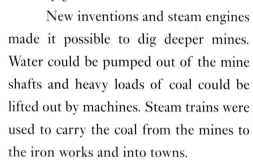

There were some mill owners who were enlightened men. Robert Owen took over a cotton mill in New Lanark. He built comfortable homes for his workers and allowed them to buy their clothes and food very cheaply at the village shop. He paid them a fair wage. No children under the age of ten could work in the factory. Instead he sent them to a free school. Very small children could go to a nursery. Adults could go to night classes. Robert Owen's business did well.

Coal Mining

Robert Owen

Coal became a more important industry during this time. Coal was needed for making glass, salt and lime. It was used for heating homes and exported overseas. Coal became the fuel which ran the newly invented steam engines. The demand for coal increased as industry grew.

New inventions and steam engines made it possible to dig deeper mines. Water could be pumped out of the mine shafts and heavy loads of coal could be lifted out by machines. Steam trains were used to carry the coal from the mines to the iron works and into towns.

Women and girls worked the mines alongside the men until 1842 when a law stopped female labour. Coal was mined in Fife, Lothians, Lanarkshire and Ayrshire. The miner's life was hard and mining villages were usually two rows of simple cottages close by the mine. Often there was no school and no church and the only shop was usually owned by the mine.

The Iron Industry

An iron works had been set up at Carron on the Firth of Forth in 1759 because it was close to forests where charcoal could be made. Charcoal was needed to smelt iron ore until Abraham Darby found a way to use coal by turning it into coke.

At Carron, cannons were made. They became known as "carronades" and were used in the wars against Napoleon. Both the Duke of Wellington and Admiral Lord Nelson preferred their weapons to be made at Carron, because they wanted the best.

The iron industries were set up close to the coal mines. The industry grew even more quickly after 1828 when James Neilson discovered how to use coal to smelt iron ore. His method was called the hot blast and it was powerful enough to smelt Scotland's supplies of blackband iron-stone. By the middle of the century over 150 Scottish furnaces were burning Scottish coal.

Life for the iron workers was just as bad as that of the mill worker and the miner. Children were used to break up the lumps of lead ore before smelting it in a furnace. When they worked at the front of the furnace they were often burned by showers of sparks and hot metal.

Shipbuilding

After the Union was formed in 1707, shipbuilding became more important. Scotland was now able to trade with colonies overseas. Sailing ships were built on the Clyde and at Leith, Dundee and Aberdeen. With the coming of steam power, however, and then steel hulls, Scotland became the foremost centre of shipbuilding in the world. The Clyde was the heart of the industry, taking orders from all over the world.

Scottish engineers designed the steam engines and boilers for ships and many of the most famous shipping lines, including Cunard and P&O, were founded by Scots.

Conditions for the Factory Worker

Large amounts of goods produced in factories meant cheaper goods to sell. Cottage industries died out because the goods produced this way were too expensive. People no longer worked at home: they went out to work. They had to work to the rules of the factory. Because there were so many people looking for work, employers often paid low wages. There were no rules about safety, health or the hours which people worked.

TRANSPORT AND COMMUNICATION
Roads

As industries grew, more goods needed to be transported from factories to cities. Heavy wagons drawn by teams of horses faced difficult journeys along narrow, muddy tracks. In wet weather the wheels sank deep into the mud. In the summer wagon axles broke over the hard stones and ruts. It made transport very expensive and much time was wasted. Even the military roads of Wade were not strong enough for the heavy wagons and teams of horses.

At the turnpike

After 1751 Turnpike Trusts were formed by local farmers and business men. They built roads and collected tolls from travellers at turnpike gates. There were hundreds of Turnpike Trusts and a new system of roads developed across the country.

Macadam

John Loudon Macadam was born in Ayrshire in 1756. He became a member of a Turnpike Trust and studied the problems of roads, rain and mud. He invented a new way of road making.

John Macadam

Instead of having flat surfaces, Macadam's roads were slightly arched higher in the centre so that rain ran off into the ditches dug at each side. The road was covered in three layers of stones with the smallest stones at the top. Traffic on the new road packed the stones down making a hard surface.

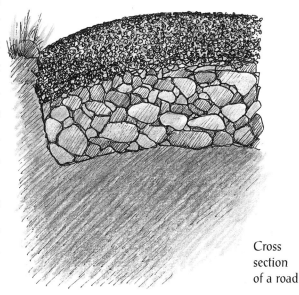

Cross section of a road

Today Macadam's method of road making is used throughout the world. The word tarmac, short for tarmacadam, is used to describe roads. Tarmacadam is a macadam road made with tar.

Telford

Thomas Telford was born in 1757 in Dumfriesshire. His father was a shepherd. He went to the local parish school and eventually became a stone mason. He worked on the building of Edinburgh's New Town before he worked in England.

In 1801 the Government asked Telford to make a report, a survey, on the communication problems in the Highlands. His ideas were so good he was given the job of making improvements. Telford was responsible for 900 miles of roads in Scotland and 120 bridges in the Highlands. He built harbours and jetties which improved fishing and ferry services. He also built the Caledonian canal which took 20 years to complete and was opened in 1822.

Thomas Telford

Canals

Other canals linked major towns and industrial centres. The Monkland Canal linked Lanarkshire coal mines with Glasgow. The Forth-Clyde Canal linked the two great rivers and enabled shipping to move across the country. The Union Canal linked Edinburgh and Falkirk while Paisley and Glasgow were also linked with a canal. Other canals were the Inverurie-Aberdeen Canal and the Crinan in the Highlands. The canals carried goods and raw materials between towns and cities. They also carried passengers.

Post Office Mail Coaches

One major improvement in communication came in 1784. The Post Office began a mail coach service which went all over Britain. The smart carriages ran to time using teams of horses which were changed every 10 miles. Mail and newspapers reached people far more quickly. The trip from London to Edinburgh took 78 hours in 1784. But by 1820 it took only 48 hours.

The Mail arrives

GOVERNMENT AND FREEDOM
Britain

Changes took place in government and the way in which the monarchy, the king or queen, ruled. Parliament became more powerful and political parties developed. They were the Tories and the Whigs. The Prime Minister's role was more important and he governed with the help of a cabinet – a group of men with special duties. The monarch could not rule without Parliament.

The change was a slow one but it made Britain very different from most other European countries where the monarch had "absolute", total power.

American War of Independence

People in the British colonies of North America wanted change too. After Britain won the Seven Years War with France all the colonies in North America were under British control. The colonies were safe from France and the people did not want to pay Britain for the British soldiers still in the colonies. Neither did they want to pay taxes to Britain. They wanted the freedom to build their own new country.

The American War of Independence began in 1775. In 1776 the colonists signed the Declaration of Independence stating that "all men are born free and equal". The war ended in 1783 and Britain lost her American colonies. Many English and Scottish settlers moved to the colonies in Canada.

American colonists fight for freedom

The French Revolution

In France, where the king ruled without a parliament, the people wanted reform. After years of war France was poor and the peasants and labourers were starving.

This developed into The French Revolution and people demanded "Liberty, Equality and Fraternity". They wanted freedom, rights and to be treated as equals. The King, Louis XVI and Queen Marie Antoinette were guillotined and, over a period of time, many French nobles were also beheaded.

French citizen's revolt

Demonstrations in Britain

In Britain there were many people who liked the ideas of freedom, equality and the right to vote. They began to demonstrate and were called Radicals by the Government. It was feared there would be a revolution in Britain. Radicals like Thomas Muir of Glasgow were put on trial and sentenced to be transported to the new colony of Botany Bay in Australia. Muir was lucky and escaped to France.

The Napoleonic Wars

The French Revolutionists raised an army and began a war with Europe. Their leader was Napoleon Bonaparte and they won many victories. Napoleon wanted to be an Emperor and to rule the countries he conquered.

He planned to conquer Britain. He was stopped by Lord Nelson who smashed the enemy fleets at the battle of Trafalgar in 1805. After this battle Britain was the greatest sea power in the world. The last battle against Napoleon was at Waterloo in Belgium in 1815. The Duke of Wellington led the British troops and, with help from the Prussians, Napoleon was finally defeated.

Many Scots fought in the Napoleonic wars. The most famous of the Highland regiments included the Cameron Highlanders, the Gordon Highlanders and the Argyll and Sutherland Highlanders.

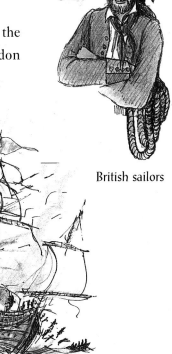

British sailors

Britain after 1815

At the end of the war the soldiers and sailors came home. It was not easy to find work. After the war, farming and industry suffered because the Army and Navy no longer needed supplies.

Caught stealing bread

In Scotland the kelp industry collapsed because cheaper products were available in other countries. Sails were no longer needed for warships and the cotton and linen factories no longer had to supply uniforms.

Life for the poor became worse because the government introduced new taxes on bread, sugar, tea, soap and tobacco. Many families had to beg in the streets and others were driven to stealing food to stay alive. Those who were caught were hanged or transported to the new colonies in Australia and New Zealand.

THE 19TH CENTURY
THE VICTORIAN AGE

In 1830 George IV died and for the next seven years his brother William was king. When he died in 1837, the granddaughter of George III became Queen of Great Britain. She was called Victoria. She was just 18 years old. She reigned for 64 years of the 19th century and saw the first year of the 20th Century. This period of history in Britain is called the Victorian Age.

Queen Victoria

Changes in Scottish Life

Life in Scotland had changed because of the revolutions in agriculture and industry. On the land Scottish inventions such as James Small's swinging plough, Patrick Bell's reaper and Andrew Meikle's threshing machines made farming more efficient. Many farm workers lost their jobs and moved to the towns or to the coal fields. By the 19th century most of Scotland's population lived in cities and towns.

Steam powered threshing machine

A steam boat

Steam Transport

Steam brought the greatest changes. Not only was steam used to work industrial machinery, it was also used for transport. The first steamboat in Scotland was called the *Charlotte Dundas* and from 1802 it worked on the Forth pulling barges. Steam boats soon carried passengers. Fishermen used steam trawlers. Steam engines brought the railway to Scotland.

THE HISTORY OF SCOTLAND FOR CHILDREN

Railways

Steam trains were first used to transport coal. In 1826 the Monkland collieries were able to transport coal to Kirkintilloch. Passenger trains soon developed. The very first one in Scotland ran between Glasgow to Garnkirk in Lanarkshire. It was driven by George Stevenson, the inventor of steam trains, on its first journey in 1831. By the middle of the century there were railways linking Britain's major towns and cities. Industries such as fishing benefited from speedy and inexpensive rail transport.

In 1879 there was a great disaster for Scotland when the Tay Bridge at Dundee collapsed as a train crossed. All the passengers and the crew lost their lives.

The Forth Rail Bridge

The great difficulties in building a rail bridge across the Firth of Forth were overcome by a team of two engineers, Sir John Fowler and Benjamin Baker and the contractor William Arrol. The Forth Rail Bridge took seven years to build and is the greatest work of 19th century British engineering. It was opened on 4 March 1890 and has become a well recognised symbol of Scotland.

Forth Rail Bridge
almost complete

A gaslit street

Gaslight

William Murdoch, (or Murdock) an Ayrshire man working in England, invented a method of producing light from coal gas. In 1803 the foundry he managed became the first industrial site lit by gas. Soon gaslight lit up factories in Scotland making working hours even longer. By the middle of the century gas was used in homes and to light up the streets of cities.

Heavy Industries

Most of Scotland's workers had jobs in heavy industry. Mining, the manufacture of iron and steel, shipbuilding and engineering were the most important industries.

Conditions for the Workers

Large factories and new industries brought great wealth to Scotland. The people who worked in these factories and industries were still poorly paid. They worked long hours in dangerous conditions. They mostly lived in the dirty slums of the great cities. In the tall tenements families shared a single room. They had no toilets and no water. They had no way to improve their living and thousands of people died because of illness and disease. Many could find no work and others turned to crime.

A Glasgow tenement with open drain

Some projects were started to provide work. In Edinburgh people were paid to clear parks and build paths on Calton Hill. There were similar projects in Glasgow and other major towns. This did not solve the problems. People demonstrated and some of these gatherings ended in riots. The Government acted harshly, determined to prevent a revolution. After a demonstration near Falkirk three weavers and miners were hanged as Radicals.

THE AGE OF REFORM

In an age of enlightenment there were some leaders who saw that changes had to be made. The years between 1815 and 1854 became known as the Age of Reform.

Voting for Members of Parliament

Change came slowly because of the way in which the Parliament and the Government were organised. Only wealthy landowners could choose members of Parliament. The rich and powerful Members of Parliament were not representing the people. Ordinary men could

Representing the people

not vote. There were demonstrations and rallies to make the Government see that changes were needed.

In 1832 the Reform Act gave the vote to a wider group of men including factory owners, and businessmen. Men who did not own land could not vote. The poor had no say in government. Women could not vote.

The Factories Act

There were men in government who worked to improve conditions for the workforce and the poor. William Wilberforce worked to have slavery abolished in British colonies. In 1833 the Factory Act made it illegal for children under nine to work. It set down the hours that young people under 18 were allowed to work.

William Wilberforce

Forty Years of Changes

In 1842 the Mines Act put a stop to women and children working in mines. In 1846 the potato crops failed and people were starving. The Corn Law which made bread so expensive was repealed, or lifted. In 1867 working men in towns and cities were given the vote. In 1872 the vote was made secret. Working men in the countryside received the vote in 1884. Women were still not allowed to vote.

Town Councils

The old burgh councils in the towns were changed too. Merchants and guildsmen were replaced by councillors elected by householders. The householders wanted changes and chose the men who would improve life in the towns.

Epidemics of cholera killed thousands of people in 1832 and during the 1840s. Hospitals such as the Royal Infirmary in Glasgow were extended to cope with fever patients. Gradually doctors and councillors began to see that dirty living conditions had to be improved. Clean water was piped into the cities from nearby lochs. Sewage and drainage pipes were laid and streets were paved.

Other changes included public baths and wash-houses. Hospitals, parks, gas street lighting, libraries and museums were also provided by the new town councils. The most important changes came when councils cleared the slums and began to build "council houses".

Robert Adam's Royal Infirmary, Glasgow

Trade Unions

During The Victorian Age workers helped themselves by forming trade unions such as the United Coal and Iron Miners' Association of Scotland. Members of these trade unions had been to parish schools. Some studied at night and were well educated. They fought for better pay and better working conditions for the workers. They also began to see that the working classes, the labourers, needed a political party of their own.

A trade union meeting

The Scottish Labour Party and James Keir Hardie

In 1888 the Scottish Labour Party was formed by James Keir Hardie. As a small boy he had to leave school to help support his family. By the age of ten he was a trapper for the mines, operating the trap which let air in underground. He studied at night and later he became a miner. He knew all about hard work and little pay. When he tried to organise a strike for better pay he lost his job and his miner's cottage. Hardie became a journalist. His interest in politics grew.

Ramsay MacDonald

He believed in a socialist form of government – a government which would treat all people fairly. Industries and farms should be owned by the nation not by private owners. He thought that wealth could then be shared and life would be better for the workers and the poor. Some of the other things he fought for included shorter working hours, better homes, fair rents, a democratic government and work for the unemployed.

Keir Hardie

In 1892 James Keir Hardie was elected a Member of Parliament. In 1893 the

Scottish Labour Party joined up with other labour societies and the Independent Labour Party was formed. Keir Hardie was the first chairman. The first secretary was also a friend of Hardie's, a Scot named Ramsay MacDonald. In 1924 Ramsay MacDonald became the first Prime Minister of Britain's first Labour Government.

Alexander
Graham Bell

LIFESTYLE

During The Victorian Age life improved for all but the very poor. Slums were cleared and cities grew larger. Horse-drawn "omnibuses" and then trams took people to and from work. The first cars appeared on Scottish roads at the turn of the century. Gas lighting and then electricity became used in most homes.

The telephone was invented by a Scot, Alexander Graham Bell, living in America in 1875. By the end of the century it was essential for business and a way of life for many Scots.

Victorian city life

Education

In 1872 an Education Act set up board schools for all children aged 5 to 13. Instead of being run by the church these schools were run by committees (boards) elected by the members of the community.

Life for the Rich

A very comfortable life

The way that people lived and worked also changed. Life for the well-to-do was very comfortable. They lived in large houses and had many servants. Some of these servants lived in the basements or attics of their employer's houses. Girls and boys from working class families often went into "service". They cooked, cleaned and looked after the houses and gardens of the wealthy folk.

New Jobs

There were new types of work as well. Shops needed assistants and hospitals needed nurses. The new board schools provided work for teachers. Women found work as telephonists at the telephone exchanges and others used the new typewriters in office jobs. Many other women worked in factories such as clothing manufacturers with poor conditions and little pay. Women still had no rights and no unions.

Days Off

As life became easier for most folk, there was time for relaxation. Golf became organised and the first Open Championship was held in 1860. Football had always been popular but in 1873 the Scottish Football Association was formed. People could travel to see their favourite teams play away. Other sports included curling and bowling. People even took holidays. It was easy to travel to the coast. Seaside holidays became popular. The bicycle brought freedom to the younger generation and cycling clubs became popular.

The Start of the Tourist Trade in Scotland

Scotland became popular. Sir Walter Scott's poems and novels were read all over the world. His descriptions of the Scottish scenery and his romantic tales of Scottish history made people want to see the countryside for themselves.

The laws against wearing the kilt were repealed after 1782. When King George IV had visited Edinburgh in 1822, Scott had persuaded him to wear tartan. In 1842 the young Queen Victoria and her husband Prince Albert visited Scotland. She bought Balmoral Castle and made Scotland the fashionable place for wealthy Victorians to visit. In 1846 Thomas Cook organised the first Tours of Scotland.

Victorian Highland "Traditions"

Because Queen Victoria was interested in the Highlands, the traditions of the Highlands became popular. Unfortunately, most of the traditions were invented by Victorians. There were fake tartans. Myths about the bagpipes were invented. The Victorians designed "The Highland Dress" which included large sporrans of fur and smartly tailored jackets. It was very different from the long, roughly woven plaid which the Highlanders used to wrap around themselves.

Victorian tourists

Life in the Highlands

While Victoria was enjoying Balmoral, the Clearances continued. Many more Highlanders left Scotland of their own free will. Some men joined the Highland Regiments to fight in the Crimean War in Russia (1854). Often those who returned found their families had been evicted, or the laird had sold their lands to the new rich industrialists from England.

It was fashionable to own a Highland estate where hunting, shooting and fishing could be enjoyed. Some Highlanders found work building the modern "castles" and country homes, while others became gamekeepers, ghillies, gardeners and foresters.

A fashionable
Highland estate

Whisky

During this period the whisky industry
developed into big business. It did not help the
Highlands. Whisky from their small distilleries
went to the Lowlands to be blended and bottled.

Aluminium

Aluminium was a new lightweight metal useful
for parts of machines and for household items

Highland
whisky
distillery

such as pots and pans. In 1896 the British Alumnium Company began production at the
Falls of Foyers on Loch Ness where they had their own hydro-electric supply of cheap
electricity. In 1907, after four years of contruction work and the making of a dam, a second
larger plant was opened at Kinlochleven near Glencoe. Scotland became one of the world's
most important producers of aluminuim within a few years.

The Crofters

Some people remained on the land. Those tenant farmers who had been removed to small
coastal plots of land still tried to make a living in the traditional way. During the 19th

A Black House

Century these small holdings became known as
"crofts". The small plots of land could only
grow enough food to keep a family living
because the original idea was that the men would
take up fishing or work in local industries.
Livestock grazed on common ground.

The crofters' homes were one or two-
roomed stone cottages. They usually had
thatched roofs and sometimes slate roofs.

Crofters made their own candles, grew their own flax and wool which they spun and made into clothes. Simple farm tools included the foot plough or hand ploughs and sledges for carting peat and manure. Few crofters could afford a horse and cart.

Crofters had few comforts

Unfair Rents and Evictions

The crofters still paid rents to the landlord and they could still be evicted. They had no rights over the land. By the middle of the century, crofters were beginning to speak out against the unfair rents and evictions. John Murdoch of Inverness began a paper called *The Highlander* which let the public know what was happening to the crofters. Gradually the Government became involved.

In Skye the landlord took away the common grazing so he could have more land for his deer. The crofters asked for their grazing to be returned. The landlord decided to get rid of trouble makers and he served eviction notices. The crofters burnt the notices and soldiers were sent in. This time, however, the general public knew what was going on because of *The Highlander*. It was unfair. The landlord had to let the crofters have their common grazing. This was only one of many such incidents.

The crofters were prepared to fight for their rights. Finally a government commission was set up to study the problems faced by crofters. Eventually the crofters gained rights which protected their lands and their way of life. It remained a hard way to earn a living. There was never enough land for those who wanted it. Highlanders continued to leave Scotland to make new lives in Australia, Canada and New Zealand.

Burning eviction notices

The Richest Country in the World

Queen Victoria died in 1901. By the end of the Victorian Age, Scotland relied upon heavy industry for her wealth. Scotland was the world's most important centre for steel production. The heavy industries of coal, iron, steel and shipbuilding kept thousands in jobs. Other industries grew up in the industrial belt stretching across central Scotland.

Oil was produced from shale and over 100 companies employed thousands of people producing lubricating oil, wax and paraffin. Singer sewing machines were produced in Glasgow and other industries included the manufacture of dynamite, chemicals and rubber.

While the rich and powerful led lives of luxury, many still lived in slums and died of disease. In between were many people who had made better lives for themselves. Britain was the richest country in the world. The British Empire included Canada, India, parts of Africa, Australia, New Zealand, islands in the Caribbean and many smaller outposts, including Hong Kong. Many Scots had emigrated to these colonies.

Old Queen
Victoria

The British
Empire

Key:
⬤ BRITISH COLONY
▨ UNDER BRITISH RULE
Is. ISLAND

THE 20TH CENTURY
THE EDWARDIAN YEARS

Edward VII became king and the next few years of British history is called Edwardian. It was the start of a new century and a time of change. The greatest change came in 1906 when there was a general election and the Liberals came to power. They had the support of the Labour MPs (Members of Parliament). Between 1906 and 1914 there were reforms which helped the old, unemployed, sick and children.

The Old Age Pension

Old folk worked until they were too weak or sick to work. Very few had been able to save money during their lives so they could not "retire". If they were lucky their families might be able to keep them. The unlucky ones went to the workhouses where hundreds lived under strict rules. There were workhouses for men and separate ones for women. Married couples were split up. The old lived in fear of being sent to these workhouses.

Edward VII

In 1909 the Old Age Pension Scheme was introduced. People could plan to retire at the age of 70 and the pension money would help to keep them out of the workhouses.

Help for the Unemployed

Unemployed people had no money to keep their families and there was no system to help them find work. In 1910 Labour Exchanges were set up to help people find work. The scheme for Unemployment Benefits, or payments, started. People in jobs paid a small amount into the scheme. So did employers and the Government. If a person lost a job then they would receive some money to help them live while they looked for a new job. This unemployment benefit became known as the dole.

Help for the Sick

A scheme for Sick Pay was started too. Money was paid by the worker, the employer and the Government into a fund. If a person was ill then they received some of this money until they could go back to work. Women received money if they were having a baby and there were free doctors and medicines for the sick.

The Children's Act

Conditions for children improved too. Free secondary schools were started, though it was still legal for 12 year olds to go out to work. There were free medical inspections and free meals in schools. Until this time children were treated as adults under the law and received the same punishments, even going to prison. In 1908 the Children's Act changed this situation and children were sent to reformatories or industrial schools rather than prisons. This Act also banned children from smoking.

GEORGE V

In 1910 Edward VII died and his son George V became king. Great changes had taken place during Edward's short reign. During this time there were strikes by dockyard workers and miners demanding better pay and better conditions. Women demonstrated for the right to vote. The first aeroplane had flown. Electricity and the telephone were more commonly used. There were electric trams and almost 10,000 motor cars were on Scottish roads. Working class families lived in better conditions with a toilet outside and a cold water tap in the kitchen. Medicine controlled the worst of the diseases, such as smallpox. Town councils started to clear the slums.

George V

KEY: ● Allied Powers.
● Neutral Countries which joined the Allies later.
● Neutral Countries.
● Central Powers.
● Neutral Countries which joined the Central Powers later.

KEY to countries :
1 HOLLAND
2 BELGIUM
3 LUXEMBOURG
4 SWITZERLAND
5 SERBIA
6 ALBANIA
7 GREECE
8 BULGARIA
9 RUMANIA

The Great War

The Build Up to War

The island nation of Great Britain was one of the most important countries in Europe and in the world at this time. However, the German Empire under Kaiser William II began to grow very strong also. Before long they were producing almost as much coal and steel as Britain. They developed new industries and built up a large navy of great battleships.

Italy and the Austro-Hungarian nation were allies of the German Empire. France and Russia were allies of Britain. In 1914 an assassin shot and killed the heir to the Austro-Hungarian throne in the Yugoslavian town of Sarajevo, then part of Austria-Hungary. The death was blamed on Serbia and war was declared.

Germany took the side of Austria-Hungary while Russia sided with the Serbs. As France prepared to support Russia, Germany quickly declared war on France moving troops through Belgium planning to take Paris. On 4 August 1914 Britain declared war on Germany.

THE FIRST WORLD WAR

The First World War lasted between 1914 and 1918 during which time over 140,000 Scottish soldiers and civilians lost their lives. The war spread through the Middle East and many lost their lives in places such as Gallipoli, where troops from Australia and New Zealand came to support Britain. America joined the Allies in 1917.

KEY: Railway
      Naval Bases
      The Border

Scotland at war

The Highlands

The British Fleet was based at Scapa Flow and other parts of the Highlands became vitally important. The railway between Perth, Inverness and Wick supplied the fleet and a second naval base was established at Invergordon.

Life in the Highlands was changed by the war. There were thousands of extra people to house and feed. Fishermen found their fishing boats were required as transport vessels and patrol boats. Those who continued to fish were at risk from mines and the torpedoes of newly developed German submarines called U-boats.

Fishing boats at Wick

The German Blockade

The German fleet blockaded Britain, attacking merchant ships and preventing goods from entering the country. The coal mines needed a supply of wooden props for the pits. When timber imports from Norway stopped there was no choice but to cut down the last of the great Caledonian Forests. Food became scarce and expensive. Supplies of food from abroad stopped because of the German blockade. In 1917 the Government introduced rationing cards so that food could be shared properly.

The Scottish War Effort

The Clyde with its shipyards and engineering factories became the most important centre for Scotland's war effort. The biggest munitions factory producing bombs, mines and bullets was also here.

Elsewhere in Scotland factories turned their efforts towards the war. Sacking for sandbags needed for the trenches was made at Dundee. Wherever there were textile factories, equipment such as tents and uniforms were being made. Aeroplanes were manufactured in Glasgow and their engines were made in Dumfries.

Battle in the Skies

Germany launched airships and bombed London and Edinburgh. By the end of the war Britain had sent its first bomber planes across Germany. Aeroplanes were first used to keep track of the enemy troop movements but fighter planes were soon developed. Plane battles in the skies were known as "dogfights".

The Home Front

On the home front women took on the jobs left by men. They were women from all classes of life. They worked in factories making bombs. This was very dangerous. They drove buses and trams and became plumbers and carpenters. They worked as engineers building tanks and guns. They joined the services to take on duties such as driving and office work. Women worked on the land. They became doctors, nurses and ambulance drivers. Many women also went to the front.

The Great War ended at the 11th hour of the 11th day of the 11th month in 1918. By the end of the war the world had changed completely.

Women at war

BETWEEN THE WARS
The Role of Women

The war had changed the role of women especially. The work they had done was recognised by the Government. In 1918 married women over 30 received the vote. In 1928 all women over 21 had the vote. After the war many middle-class women stayed at school and went to university. However, life for the poor had been made worse by the war. Many women were war widows and were left with families to support by themselves.

Gaining a degree

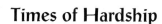

War widow

Times of Hardship

Men returned from the war to find there was no work. In 1919 there was little fuel for homes and food was in short supply. An epidemic of influenza made three out of four people ill and there were thousands of deaths.

The 1920s and 1930s were times of hardship. There was a drop in world trade and Scotland was badly affected. After the war, Scottish goods were not required by countries which had developed their own industries. Coal and iron deposits were running out in some areas. Many Scottish companies became part of British or American companies and when the slump came, the Scottish factories were closed down. Fewer ships were needed and unemployment led to great hardships on Clydeside.

Between 1925 and 1934, 25 out of every 100 people were out of work in Scotland. There were strikes and hunger marches to make the Government realise how desperate the people felt.

The Scottish National Party was formed in 1932 and it fought to have a Scottish Government which would represent Scotland better than the Government based in London.

Many Scots moved to England in search of work and thousands emigrated.

Thousands emigrated

Edward VIII

1936 and two Kings

George V died in 1936 and his eldest son, Edward became King. However, he gave up the throne, abdicated, before the end of the year because he wanted to marry an American, Mrs Wallace Simpson. She had been married before and the British Parliament could not allow her to become queen.

Edward's brother became King George VI.

George VI

Mrs Simpson

Lifestyle

For those who had work, the 1920s and 1930s brought a better standard of living. Electricity gradually replaced gas and coal as a form of heating and light. The radio brought entertainment and news into almost every household. The cinema was a popular form of entertainment with special "matinee" shows during the day for children. New electrical appliances such as vacuum cleaners, washing machines, stoves and refrigerators appeared in the shops. Few people could afford such luxuries. There were new council homes being built and those who could afford to bought their own new homes.

Listening to the radio

Transport and Communication

Cars became cheaper and many middle class families owned a car. This meant they could get out into the countryside. Businesses used vans and lorries to transport goods. Motor buses provided public transport to rural areas and made life easier for villages which had no train service. Tram services in the cities meant people working in the centres could live on the edges of the city. Cities grew bigger.

A new bungalow

In 1933 the first passenger flight in Scotland went from Inverness via Wick to Orkney. Soon a network of flights linked the Scottish Islands with the mainland. Journeys which had taken all day by boat were taking only minutes by plane. Before long the mail was carried by plane and an air ambulance service was set up.

Council housing

With telephones people could keep in touch with each other and a telephone was essential for business. The post was delivered to each house. Telegrams brought urgent news whatever the time of day. Newspapers and radios kept people throughout the country informed of events in Britain and across the world.

Much of the world news was about Adolf Hitler in Germany, and his plans to invade European countries which would then become part of Germany.

THE SECOND WORLD WAR

After the horrors of the First World War no one really wanted a war with Germany. However, Hitler's powerful armies marched across Europe and took Poland and on 3 September 1939, Britain declared war on Germany. In 1940 Norway and Denmark fell. Then Hitler attacked Holland, Belgium and France.

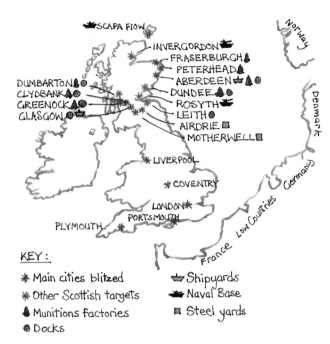

In August 1940, "The Battle of Britain" began. Hitler intended to "blitz" Britain's most important cities, London, Portsmouth, Plymouth, Coventry, Liverpool and Clydebank. About 60,000 ordinary people lost their lives. Hitler's invasion was stopped by the bravery of the fighter pilots of the Royal Air Force. Food and supplies were able to reach Britian because of the RAF Coastal Command and the Royal Navy. British Armed Forces fought in many places around the world. Italy, and then Japan became enemies. America joined the Allies after the bombing of Pearl Harbour in December 1941.

The Home Front

The war in Europe lasted from 1939 to 1945. Everyone was part of the war effort and there was no difference in the treatment between rich and poor people. Clothes and food were rationed. Many children were evacuated from the cities to safer homes in the countryside. Women took over the work of the men who joined the services and many of them joined up as well. Older people joined the Home Guard and were trained to fight if there was an invasion.

Winston Churchill

The merchant navy was heavily attacked by U-boats and by the end of the war 32,000 merchant seamen had lost their lives in battle to keep supply lines to Britain open.

Scotland Bombed

The coming of the Second World War opened up the factories again. When Scotland was bombed, Clydeside's factories and shipyards were the main targets for German bombs. The first raid came in March 1941. Clydebank was blitzed. Aside from damage to the factories there was terrible destruction to homes and over 1,000 civilians were killed. But the people were not beaten. Within a few weeks the factories were back at work.

Scapa Flow was again the base for the Royal Fleet. On 13 October 1939 a German submarine entered Scapa Flow and sank the battleship Royal Oak. Over 800 men died. To protect the fleet from further attacks, the Prime Minister, Winston Churchill, ordered

A Clydebank
tenement bombed

great barriers to be built. They are still in place today and are called the Churchill barriers. Scapa Flow later became a target for German bombers.

On 16 October German bombers attacked the shipping on the Firth of Forth. Scotland's two fighter squadrons were the first to fight a successful action in British skies. A German plane was hit and went down in the Forth.

Tom Johnston

In 1941 Winston Churchill appointed Tom Johnston as Secretary of State for Scotland. He was given a free hand to do whatever was needed to help the Scots during the war. In 1943 he set up the North of Scotland Hydro-Electric Board. He set up the Scottish Council on Industry to work with the Government, winning many contracts for Scotland. He organised free health care for the workers in the Clyde valley. Later the system extended to other parts of Scotland. Rent tribunals were set up to make sure that landlords only charged fair rents. Tom Johnston was also able to promote a separate Scottish Tourist Board – not something you may think of during a war. He was a man of great vision.

Tom Johnston

Scotland's War Effort

The River Clyde was Britain's main port, landing thousands of tons of munitions and sending thousands of troops around the world. Not only were ships built there but also the special landing piers which were needed for the invasion of Normandy on D-Day. There were factories making explosives and ammunition and the Rolls Royce factory made engines for the RAF

Border woollen mills made uniforms and Dundee's jute mills made sacking for sandbags. There was urgent need for Scottish coal, steel and iron.

Britain had become the headquarters for freedom fighters and the governments of many of Europe's occupied countries. The Highlands became the training grounds for soldiers from occupied countries like Poland and the tough mountains were used by American Commandos for training also.

Scotland's greatest contribution to the war effort was the Scots themselves. They dug up gardens to grow food, they fought

The Home Front

fires, nursed the sick and looked after evacuated children. They worked in factories and fought wherever they were sent around the world.

The war in Europe ended on 8 May 1945 and Japan surrendered on 14 August. 57,720 Scottish lives had been lost. Like their ancestors, they had fought for freedom.

Celebrating the end of war

LIFE AFTER THE WAR
Elections and Government

After the war people voted for a Labour Government which had promised a fair system of Social Security and a National Health Service. People who had fought as equals in the war wanted to be treated as equals after the war. The Labour Government "nationalised", or took

Stone of Destiny missing

control of, the main industries such as the coal mines and the railways. The Government hoped to keep people employed this way. Some new industries came to Scotland but many felt that not enough was being done.

In 1949 there was a petition for a Scottish Parliament. As a way of drawing attention to Scotland's past and her current problems, the Stone of Destiny was stolen from the Coronation Throne at Westminster Abbey. It was missing for about two years.

In the election of 1951 Scots voted equally between Conservatives and Labour but a Conservative Government took control since the rest of Britain gave them the majority votes.

In 1952 George VI died and Great Britain once again had a queen on the throne, Elizabeth II.

Lifestyle

In the following years, the differences between daily life for working class families and middle class families almost disappeared. The "class" system, or method of grouping types of people was gradually breaking down. More women worked because they wanted to, not because they had to. Children stayed at school until they were 16 and the word "teenager" was invented. Young people had a "pop" culture of their own.

The television was invented by a Scot, John Logie Baird, and became the major source of news and entertainment in the home.

There was real improvement in housing. New towns were built to provide decent houses with gardens built away from main roads. The towns were planned with parks, facilities such as libraries and doctors' clinics and shopping centres. In a separate area at the edge of the town was the industrial estate. Some of these towns are East Kilbride, Irvine, Cumbernauld, Glenrothes and Livingston New Town.

Elizabeth II

The Decline in Industry

Scotland's industries faced great changes after the war. For a while the shipyards were kept busy replacing ships lost in the war. Heavy industries supplied trains and other goods around the world until the late 50s. After this, shipyards and other industrial works began to close down because cheaper ships were made in other countries. Japan and Germany had rebuilt modern efficient industries. There were new methods of manufacturing and Scotland was behind the times.

THE SIXTIES

Dounreay

By the 60s Scotland was no longer the leading manufacturing centre for the UK. Air travel was replacing sea travel and the Clyde suffered. The Government tried to encourage other new industries in Scotland. Many found work in the electronics industry. A car plant was opened near Paisley. Dounreay in Caithness was started

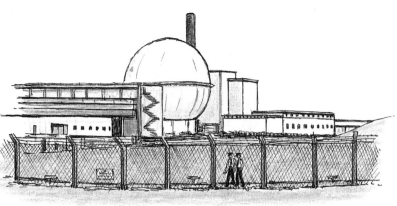

as a nuclear reactor, and an aluminium smelter opened in Invergordon. A new steelworks was built at Ravenscraig. Not all of these were successful and workers often went out on

strike for better pay or better working conditions. Investors in new manufacturing businesses preferred to set up in the Midlands in England, closer to trade in the south.

Ravenscraig

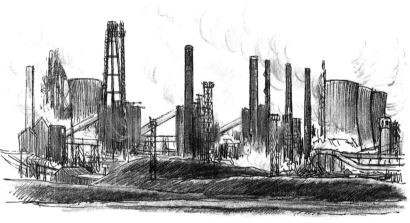

By the end of the 60s the Scottish coal industry was in trouble. Out of 71 pits, 23 had been closed down. Scottish coal became more expensive than English coal and they lost customers.

The Highlands and Islands Development Board was set up in 1965 and it helped Highlanders develop industries such as fishing and boat building. It has also helped in developing the tourist industry in the Highlands.

THE SEVENTIES

In 1970 oil was discovered in the North Sea off the Scottish coast. A new industry began. By the end of the 70s oil was the biggest industry in Scotland. It especially affected the east coast towns and Shetland, bringing new wealth. Aberdeen became the centre for the business companies involved in oil.

The oil industry provided a large number of jobs. Rigs had to be built, housing had to be provided and a helicopter service was needed to get men to and from the rigs. People employed in the industry came from many parts of Scotland.

A Scottish Assembly?

During the 60s, the Scottish National Party became stronger. Some people felt that Scotland's difficulties and unemployment problems were not likely to be resolved by a government in London. The importance of oil was used by the SNP to make voters realise "It's Scotland's Oil." Two things happened to help the SNP campaign for a Scottish Assembly. There was a war in the Middle East in 1973. Oil from there was expensive and in short supply, and in 1974 there was a strike by the coal miners in Scotland. There were two general elections. Voters were confused. The SNP increased their MPs and the Government had to take notice of them.

Despite of the oil industry, unemployment in Scotland increased. Taxes were high and the Government needed the support of the SNP to stay in power. Labour agreed to consider a Scottish Assembly.

A Referendum was held so that Scottish voters could decide what to do. Not enough voters used their rights and only one third voted "Yes". It seemed that some areas were not convinced that an Assembly would help far-off parts of the country. The Assembly would have no control over the economy. People felt problems like unemployment would remain the same.

There was another general election in May 1979. Though Scotland voted mostly Labour, the rest of the country voted mostly Conservative. Margaret Thatcher became the first female Prime Minister of Great Britain.

THE EIGHTIES

There were many troubled years as the Conservatives stopped supporting the nationalised industries which were failing. There were strikes. Britain found it was difficult to sell goods abroad and they could not compete with imported goods. Many factories closed down or reduced their work forces. Unemployment was high, especially in Scotland.

Margaret Thatcher

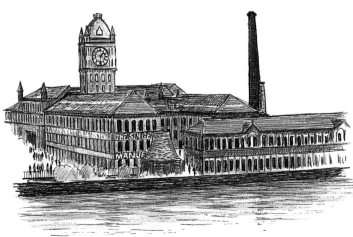

In 1980 the Singer Sewing Machine factory in Clydebank closed. At one time it had been the world's largest factory, employing 23,000 people. Modern sewing machines used micro-chips and Singer made them in other, more modern, factories. In 1981 almost 5,000 people lost their jobs when the car factory at Linwood closed down. In 1982 the Aluminium

smelter at Invergordon and Scotland's oldest company, Carron Iron Works, closed down. At this time one person out of every six in Scotland was unemployed.

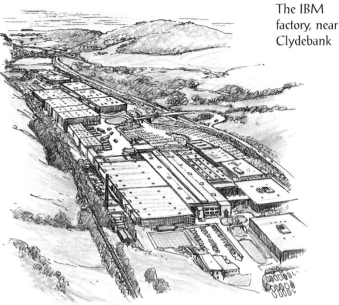
The IBM factory, near Clydebank

The 70s and 80s had brought other types of industries to Scotland. Electronics works such as Ferranti made parts for aircraft, satellites and radar systems. IBM and other computer companies brought more work to Scotland. By the mid 80s data processing equipment was Scotland's main export. The Government assisted by providing modern industrial parks and low rents. Still, unemployment remained high.

Some Scots still felt that Scotland had not done well under the Government at Westminster and they wanted a Scottish Parliament or even an Independent Scotland.

Protestors after the General Election 1992

THE NINETIES

Problems at the end of the century were much the same as those at the start of the century. Unemployment, poverty and homelessness as well as education and healthcare remained issues to be resolved.

Lifestyle

Life for the majority of Scots improved over the years. The terms "working classes" and the "middle classes" to describe people became less used. There were fewer differences in the way people lived. The rich might have had bigger houses but everyone's house had a bathroom, toilet and kitchen. There were the same opportunities in education and jobs for the children of factory workers as for the children of university professors. Of course, life is usually easier for those without money worries.

Home Life

More Scots owned their own homes during the 90s. Washing machines, refrigerators and vacuum cleaners were no longer luxuries. Homes had all sorts of electrical appliances to make life easier. The microwave oven was probably the most useful invention for the kitchen. Televisions were in most homes and there were videos as well. Many people owned computers.

Children of the 90s

Transport and Communication

By the mid 90s Scotland had lost many of the smaller railway routes. This was partly because fewer people lived in the countryside and partly because these routes were losing money. On the other hand, rail travel between main cities improved with faster electric trains. By the mid 90s the Government had sold the railways to private companies.

The increasing numbers of cars on the roads became a serious problem. Most cities planned schemes to encourage more people to use public transport.

Since the 70s there have been enormous changes in communication. There are mobile telephones. Fax machines send copies of written material across the world instantly. Computers allow people to send e-mail messages. The Internet gives access to worldwide information and communication.

Industry, Employment and the EEC

Scotland continues to attract new industry. Foreign companies have set up factories because there is a good work force. It is also close to Europe. Britain is a member of the EEC, the European Economic Community, which is set up to help European countries trade with each other. Traditional industries such as fishing have been affected by the rules of the EEC.

The tourist
industry

Tourism is one of Scotland's more important industries. People come from all over the world to visit Scottish cities and towns and to see the beautiful scenery. Many people find work in the "service" industries like hotels, restaurants and transport because of the tourists. Tourists spend money on travelling, and activities such as skiing, walking, and climbing. They buy Scottish goods such as woollen clothes and crafts.

Scottish Culture

Poets, playwrights, authors, artists, musicians, singers, dancers, film-makers and sportsmen have all contributed to the wealth of Scotland and the world. There are dozens of great authors. JM Barrie gave the world *Peter Pan*. Irvine Welsh is famous for *Trainspotting*.

Scotland has its own Scottish Ballet Company, Scottish Opera and Scottish National Orchestra as well as the BBC Scottish Symphony. There are Scottish pop groups and composers.

The Edinburgh International Festival was established in 1947 and is one of the world's largest festivals for music, dance and drama.

Film-making in Scotland is being encouraged by grants from the Lottery Fund and overseas companies are attracted to Scotland by its wealth in historical settings and dramatic scenery.

Charles
Rennie
Mackintosh

J M Barrie

There have been many great Scottish artists over the past century. "Schools" of artists painting in the same styles include *The Glasgow Boys* and *The Colourists*. Perhaps one of the better known artists was Charles Rennie Mackintosh who was also an architect working at the turn of the century. MacIntosh's distinctive designs remain popular today.

Sport is an increasingly important part of Scottish culture. Football remains as popular as it has been through the centuries and names such as Kenny Dalgleish are legendary. Golf is synonymous with Scotland and the World Golf Champion was Scot Colin Montgomery in 1996. Other traditional Scottish sports include curling and shinty while Highland Games take place around the world. Scottish sportsmen and women have taken their place among the world's greatest. These include Liz McColgan, the marathon runner, and North Queensferry's Stephen Hendry, seven times World Snooker Champion.

SCOTLAND APPROACHING THE 21ST CENTURY
1997

1997 saw four major events which linked the Scots with their past history.

At the beginning of the year the Stone of Destiny was removed from the Coronation Throne at Westminster Abbey and returned to Scotland after 700 years. It arrived at Coldstream on the Border and was marched back into Scotland with great ceremony. The Stone of Destiny will return to Westminster for future Coronations, since it is an important part of the traditions in "making a king".

The Stone of Destiny returned to Scotland

For many years the Island of Eigg had been owned by one rich person after another and these landlords had done little for the islanders who lived there. In 1997 the islanders took control of their own destiny and bought the island of their ancestors for themselves.

In May 1997 there was a general election. In many previous elections Scottish votes were outweighed by votes from England and Wales. In this election Scotland did not return one single Conservative MP. The majority of voters in England and Wales also voted Labour.

In September of the same year there was another referendum. The Scottish people had the chance to decide if they wanted a Scottish Parliament and also if they wanted it to have tax-raising powers. This time they voted "Yes".

1998

In 1998 Westminster Parliament worked out the details of a new Scottish Parliament in the Scotland Bill. They agreed on all the areas which would be controlled by Scotland, for example education, health, law and order and housing. They decided on the numbers of MPs. They worked out a new system of voting which means that all parts of Scotland have

a fair chance of electing the MPs and the type of government they want. The Bill received the Royal Assent in November 1998 and became the Scottish Act.

It was decided to build a new Scottish Parliament building at the end of the Royal Mile, near Holyrood Palace. There was an international competition for the best designs. The designs of Enric Miralles from Barcelona were chosen and he teamed up with architects from Edinburgh to complete the project.

On 2 March 1999, Knoydart Foundation were successful in their long campaign to buy the estate for the people of Knoydart. This isolated mountainous estate had been "cleared" in 1853 and sold many times. Since 1945 the estate has had seven different owners. Now it is owned by those who live there.

1999

On 6 May 1999 elections were held for the Scottish Parliament and the first meeting was held on 12 May when MPs took their oaths.

The Scottish Parliament opened officially on 1 July 1999.

Scotland gave itself the opportunity to control the welfare of its citizens. The difficulties of the 21st Century will be the same as those of the past. People will need work, homes, healthcare and education. The challenge will be for Scots to achieve all this for themselves.

INDEX

THE HISTORY OF SCOTLAND FOR CHILDREN

GLOSSARY OF SCOTTISH WORDS AND SELECTED TERMINOLOGY

Wherever possible the author has explained the meanings of "less familiar" words in context.

Abbey	The church and buildings where monks or nuns live and work with an Abbot or Abbess in charge.
Abbot	A Churchman. The head of an abbey and its monks.
Alliance	A partnership to protect each other.
Archaeologist	A person who studies artifacts from the past.
Archbishop	A Churchman. The chief bishop.
Architect	A person who designs buildings.
Assassin	A traitor who murders a king or other important person.
Artillery	Small cannons on wheels which could be taken into battle by horses.
Artisans	Craftsmen.
Auld	Old.
Auld Alliance	The traditional partnership between Scotland and France against their auld enemy, England.
Bagpipes	The Highland bagpipes are played by blowing air into a sack and then squeezing it out through the drones, pipes which make the long droning sounds, and the chanter which is played by the piper to produce the notes of the music. There are Lowland and Border bagpipes which are played differently.
Bannocks	Flat cakes.
Bayonets	Rifles with long knife blades attached.
Bishop	A Churchman. Higher than a priest, he is in charge of a district and other priests.
Bonnie	Good-looking.
Borders, The	The areas immediately north of the English border.
Brewing	Making ale or beer.
Burn	A stream.
Byre	A barn.
Cardinals	A Churchman, appointed by the Pope to represent him and to rule the Catholic Church outside Rome.
Catholics	Those Christians following the teachings and rules of the church headed by the Pope in Rome.
Cavalry	Soldiers riding horses.
Charcoal	Made from partly burning wood in ovens.

Chariot	A two wheeled cart, pulled by horses and used in fighting.
Clan	A family group or tribe.
Colleries	Coal mines.
Commission	An official group of people with certain powers and duties.
Compensation	Something paid back to make up for a wrong doing.
Convention of Estates	A meeting of parliament made up of the three "estates" or classes, i.e. nobles, landowners and burgesses.
Cottar	A farmworker.
Currency	System of money.
Custom Duties	A tax paid on goods brought into the country.
Dauphin	The son and heir of the French King.
Dean	The head of a cathedral, or important church.
Democratic	Elected by the people.
Demons	Devils, evil spirits.
Divine	Of God, God-given.
Dragoons	Foot soldiers, or infantry who rode to the place of battle on horses.
Emigration	Leaving one's homeland to settle in another land.
Epidemics	The spreading of a disease throughout a town or even country.
Estates	Large areas of land sometimes including villages and farms.
Exiled	Sent away from one's homeland.
Famine	A time when there is very little food.
Feuds	Disagreements between families or clans often lasting many years and sometimes ending in bloodshed.
Gaelic	Language of the Scottish Celts.
Gamekeepers	People who breed and conserve game birds such as pheasants and grouse for the estate.
Ghillies	Assistants for sportsmen, either for fishing or deer stalking.
Glens	Valleys.
Guidman	Goodman: the way that people who were equals would greet a stranger, who was not a peasant or servant. A guidman was the head of a household and usually had a small piece of land.
Harness	The leather straps which allows a chariot to be hitched to a horse.
Heather	A tough plant which survives on the mountains and hills: usually with purple or white flowers.
Herring	A fish from the North Atlantic seas.
Highlands	The areas, including the Islands, where Gaelic was spoken: roughly, the regions above and west of the plains of Aberdeen, including the Grampian Mountains and across to Dumbarton.
Journalist	A person who writes for a newspaper or magazine.

Jousting	Knights on horses ride against each other with long spears.
Kilt	Not a Scottish word, but now used to describe the modern pleated tartan skirt. Originally a long piece of woollen cloth was "kilted up", tucked up around the waist and the rest went over the shoulders. It was also used as a blanket or "quilt".
Kirks	Churches of Scotland run without bishops.
Laird	A landowner - usually of an estate and a house.
Lichen	A plant which spreads on rocks, tree trunks, roofs, etc. and is usually grey, green or yellow.
Linen	Cloth made from flax, a plant which produces fibres which can be spun and then woven.
Loch	Lake.
Lowlands	The areas where Scots rather than Gaelic was spoken: roughly, an area including the coastal plains of Aberdeen, south of the Grampian Mountains and across to Dumbarton.
Mass	A service in the Catholic church.
Matinee	Afternoon shows.
Minstrels	Musicians.
Monarch	A king or queen.
Monastry	The place where monks lives.
Monk	A churchman who lives his life serving God under strict rules, often cut off from the world.
Moor	Open wasteland often covered with heather.
Mourned	Felt sad or sorry.
Munitions	Any military equipment including ammunition, i.e. bombs and bullets.
Musket	An early type of hand gun.
Oath	A promise made in the name of God.
Peat	Plants which have rotted in boggy ground and which is dug out in blocks, dried and used for fuel.
Persecution	The tracking down and punishment of people for their beliefs.
Plantations	Large estates where cotton, tobacco or sugar was grown and where slaves were used in the past.
Pope	The head of the Catholic church: he rules from Rome.
Preacher	A teacher of religion.
Priest	A churchman who looks after the people belonging to a church: takes the church services and tells the people about God.
Presbyterian	The church formed after the Reformation, ruled by elders and ministers who are all equal.
Principal	The most important or main thing.

Protestants	Those Christians who broke away from the Catholic church to form another church.
Psalm	A hymn or song from the Bible.
Quern	Stones which can be turned by hand to grind corn into flour.
Ransom	Money paid to free a person.
Referendum	A government's system for allowing voters to decide an important issue by voting, usually yes or no to a question.
Regent	The person who rules in place of a king or queen.
Sacred	Something precious or important to a religion.
Saltire	The X-shaped cross used on shields and flags: the white cross on a blue background is the cross of St Andrew, Patron Saint of Scotland.
Shale	Soft clay-type stones.
Siege	The type of warfare when an army camps around a fortress, cutting off supplies, forcing the defenders to give up.
Social Security	A Government system to look after people who are in difficulty with work or housing, etc.
Superstitious	Fear of the unknown, mysterious or supernatural.
Tanning	Turning animal skins into leather.
Tapestries	Woven cloth stitched with pictures usually hung on walls.
Tavener	The man who runs a tavern suppling food and drink.
Tax	Money or goods paid to the king or government.
Tenant	A person who pays money, i.e. rent for the use of land and or housing.
Textile	Woven cloth.
Torc	A necklace or bracelet of twisted metal, usually gold or silver.
Traitor	A person who is not loyal to the king or country.
Tram	A passenger carriage which runs along rails, first drawn by horses and later on run on electricity.
Treasury	The place where tax money is kept for the king or government.
Treaty	An agreement.
Tribunals	Law courts set up to judge on certain matters.
Troops	Large units of soldiers.
Tropics	The very hot lands just north and south of the equator.
Union	Joining up.
Wynds	Narrow alleyways between buildings.

SELECTED BIBLIOGRAPHY

My role in writing this book has been that of Storyteller. My sources are secondary and there have been many of them. I hope the authors of these books, those who worked from original sources, will find one day that young readers of this volume are inspired to read their works.

From the many titles to which I have referred, I list below, those which I hope adult readers may find informative, accessible and intriguing. Many are well-known standard works.

The Edinburgh History of Scotland – Four Volumes – Mercat Press

A History of Scotland – JD Mackie – Pelican

Scotland – A New History – Michael Lynch – Century

Scotland in the 20th Century – Edited by TM Devine & AJ Finlay – EUP

The New History of Scotland – Edited by Jenny Wormald – Edward Arnold

Collins Encyclopedia of Scotland – Edited by John Keay & Julia Keay – Harper Collins

Historical Atlas of Britain – Edited by M Falkus, J Gillighan – Book Club Associates

Scotland in the 20th Century – Edited by TM Devine & RJ Finlay – EUP

Scotland's War – Seona Robertson & Les Wilson – Mainstream Publishing

This Present Emergency – Andrew Jeffrey – Mainstream Publishing

A New History of Scotland – Eric Melvin, Ian Gould & John Thompson – John Murray

Scotland's Story – Tom Steel – A Channel Four Book – Collins

Life in Scotland – Norman Nichol – A & C Black

Picts – Anna Ritchie – HMSO

Prehistoric Orkney – Anna Ritchie – Batsford/Historic Scotland

Scotland BC – Anna Ritchie – HMSO

Scotland's First Settlers – CR Wickham-Jones – Batsford/Historic Scotland

Nechtansmere 1300 – Graeme Cruickshank – Forfar & District Historical Society

Pennant's Tour of Scotland – 3 Volumes

Old and New Edinburgh – 3 Volumes

Titles by TC Smout, Nigel Tranter and John Prebble.

Various titles published by HMSO, Historic Scotland (Batsford), and The National Trust.